ALL ALONE

JOE PAYNE

BRITISH HOME CHILD

A NOVEL

CAROLYN ANNE MACISAAC
AUTHOR OF *THE DAY MY WORLD STOOD STILL*

Copyright
All rights reserved
ISBN 978-0-359-78589-6
Published by Lulu Press, Inc

No part of this book may be used or reproduced in any manner whatsoever without the prior written permission of the publisher, except in the case of brief quotations embodied in reviews.

Joseph Payne was born during the Industrial Revolution in England in 1905. It was a time of great poverty. Britain had too many starving and orphaned children in crowded cities, and Canada had acres and acres of green fields and a need for farm workers. When World War 1 broke out in 1914, Joe became one of 100,000 British Home Children sent to Canada and indentured to work on a farm until he was eighteen years of age.

All Alone Again is Joe's story. His daughter, Carolyn Anne MacIsaac has used all the information and all the pictures and postcards she could find about her Dad and his family and woven a tale around it. Times were hard in both England and Canada in the early 20th century. There is a saying *"You did then what you knew how to do, and when you knew better you did better."**

Carolyn Anne MacIsaac, a British Home Child Descendant, is on the board of directors for the British Home Children and Descendants Association, Nova Scotia. Carolyn studied literature through Mount Allison University, New Brunswick and has an Associate of Arts Diploma and a Diploma in Social work from Waterloo University, Ontario. She resides in Pictou County, Nova Scotia with her husband of fifty five years. They have three children and six grandchildren.

Other books by Anne MacIsaac
The Day My World Stood Still a story of the author's eight months in Alberta while her son underwent a bone marrow transplant for leukemia
A Little Child Shall Lead Them a novel for Young People

*Quote by Maya Angelou

This book is dedicated to all the British Home Children who came to Canada between 1869 and 1939. You not only survived, you thrived. Today we, your descendants, proudly make up at least 13% of all Canadians.

Thank you to my cousin, Joe Bumford, in England, for all your research and the photos and postcards you sent.

Thank you to The Write Intentions of Pictou County for encouraging me and proof reading my book.

Special thanks to my editor Heather MacInnis, who knows where commas belong.

Thanks to Catherine West, Chair for British Home Children and descendants Nova Scotia for her letter of recommendation.

> Carolyn,
> I thoroughly enjoyed reading your book. You certainly know how to make your father's life real to the reader. I love how you explain historical facts as you go along. It sets the scenes so well that I had no trouble visualizing them.
> This book will definitely sell to any Home Child descendant who gets a chance to see it. I want to be one of your first customers. I give it my whole-heated recommendation.
> Catherine

Most of all, thanks to my husband, Eldridge, for not only his patience with all the hours I spent doing research and writing this book, but also his knowledge of farming and working in a lumber camp.

WHY THE SUNFLOWER
(Flower that represents British Home Children)

Sunflowers are bright and inspire hope.

British Home Children came to Canada hoping for a brighter future.

As the sunflower grows, the flowers and leaves grow and face the sun in order to maximize photosynthesis. On sunny days, the stems elongate on the side of the stem away from the sun. The immature (young) flowers and leaves follow the light of the sun throughout the day. By the end of the day, the immature flowers are facing the west. When there is no light, the other side of the stem grows and pushes the flower and leaves back to face the east at sunrise. This is otherwise known as heliotropism. Mature flowers, leaves and plant do not turn to follow the light of the sun.

British Home Children got off their ships in the east and most travelled west into all parts of Canada.

Sunflowers are very strong and can endure various environments

British Home Children had to be strong mentally, physically and emotionally and endured various living situations.

Sunflower seeds are encased in shells.

British Home Children on the most part kept their stories of their lives to themselves, encasing them within their hearts, minds & souls.

Sunflower seeds can be cracked open to reveal itself for others to share and appreciate.

British Home Children stories need to be cracked open, shared and appreciated.

Poem printed by permission from Judy Neville, the Ontario East British Home Child Family group.

The banner atop the crest reads HOME CHILDREN CANADA which suggests that our interest is national and includes all children sent from the four dozen or more agencies in the UK to Canada and former colonies and dominions as well as their families in the UK or elsewhere.

- The LION AGAINST A FIELD OF RED represents the sending country - the Mother country.

- The SILHOUETTE OF THE URBAN INDUSTRIAL CENTRE suggests the places from which most poor child migrants came.

- The SHIP GUIDED BY THE STAR OF GOOD HOPE brought the children west.

- The GOLDEN SKY, MOUNTAINS, FIELDS, RIVERS AND SHEATHS OF WHEAT represent the promise of the children's new home - the wide open spaces and food a-plenty.

- The FALL MAPLE LEAF AGAINST A FIELD OF WHITE is our national emblem and colours.

- The motto is in age-old Latin: SPIES IN CANADA and means OUR HOPE IS IN CANADA.

SOME INFORMATION REGARDING CHILDREN
FROM THE MIDDLEMORE HOME, FAIRVIEW STATION, HALIFAX, N S
J.STERLING KING, MANAGER

The Training Home is in Birmingham England. Children are brought out about June first every year. A few boys and girls from other Training Homes come with ours. They are from 1 to 18 years old but the majority are 5 to 12 years of age. The younger ones give the better satisfaction. They more readily adapt themselves to their new homes. *They are Protestant and settled in Protestant homes only.* They are mostly, English, taken from families that have lost mother or father or both, but from families of as good character, breeding and respectability as possible. We cannot afford to bring out those whom we know will prove unsatisfactory, but in spite of our care a few do turn out badly. Those who cannot be corrected or improved are returned to England. Very seldom do we have to do this. We have settled nearly 5000 children in Canada and not over 2 per cent have proved total failures. Any child not satisfactory is removed. We try to visit at least once a year. We need "homes" not "situations" good influences, proper trailing - strictness with kindness,-a chance for the younger ones to *attend school* and for all to attend *Sunday School and Church. Services.* We have legal control as Guardian until they are 21 unless sooner married, but at 18 they are given a certain amount of freedom, provided they are in good homes, conduct themselves properly and are capable of taking proper care of themselves. We settle them in all good localities in New Brunswick, Nova Scotia and P. E. Island. At present, besides looking after the home and the rapidly increasing office work, we have about 1000 children to visit, special calls to attend etc.

The selection of homes and children for them is made before the Boat arrives. A cable message is received from Newfoundland and notice is sent to each successful applicant when and where to meet the child. *Children cannot be picked on landing—there is no time.* They must pass Inspectors, Doctors etc., and get their papers, - baggage must be landed, sorted, checked and placed on different trains. Tickets must be purchased, children fed and cared for over night at the comfortable quarters in the Immigration Shed and the right parties got ready for each train. As a rule there are three large parties made up, each having a car to themselves and in charge of the English Secretary Mr. Jackson, the matrons and the manager. A list must be made for the baggage man for checks, one for the ticket agent for tickets and lists for each overseer of a party. At various junctions small parties are put in care of friends who see them safely to the several stations on the branch lines. One car is attached to the night train for St. John. From there in the morning children are set down at various stations as far as Victoria County.

The other two cars are attached to the morning trains and put down children from Halifax to Sydney and from Truro to St. John. The 150 to 175 children are generally all on the way in from 20 to 30 hours and all settled the third day after landing.

The children take some time to get used to our ways and customs. They are little strangers in a strange land and we ask for patience and kindness also strictness and correction. But more are spoiled by too much of the first than by too much of the latter. The proper religious, educational and social teaching and training of these children is a great responsibility, but we believe that those who thus benefit and bless the children will in return receive a blessing. The children's future for weal or for woe in this world and in the next, is to a large extent, in the hands of the people with whom they are placed.

Mr. Frank A. Gerow, one of our most successful managers, secured the passage of uniform laws for immigrant children in the three Maritime provinces. On these our agreement is based, under them we can remove children, proceed for neglect, ill treatment, interference etc. Each child is settled under the agreement which however does not prevent their growing up as one of the family, provided everything continues satisfactory. Very seldom is legal adoption allowed. Any change in the child's name cannot be made without the consent of the Home Manager.

THE AGREEMENT

The Form when filled in, signed and returned is filed as an application. In all cases where the applicant is unknown to the Manager or his Agent proper investigation and enquiries are made. If a boy or girl is sent, the application becomes an agreement. It binds lightly as regards keeping a child if not satisfied with it, but it is expected that the other provisions will be strictly observed. Seldom do we find the children not getting enough good, wholesome food. It is expected that they will eat at table as one of the family, except in cases where employed as hired help when other household regulations may obtain. Care should be taken that they do not overeat during the first year in Canada, or sore's, boils and eczema may result. We do find children with insufficient clothing, particularly underclothing in winter. We know they are, like most children, hard on clothing and-boots. Mended clothes are no disgrace if they are neat and clean and enough of them. Nearly every child likes and all should have a good outfit for Church and Sunday School. We cannot be expected to leave a child where the master or mistress cannot or will not properly feed or reasonably good and comfortably clothe it. We also find a large number of the children do not attend school or only for a short time. *We have therefore decided to remove all children whose names do not appear on the School register or who have failed to make the required 5 months attendance* unless we have been notified of, or find good and sufficient reasons.

They must have a chance to attend school when young for when they grow up they will be expected to work. When done at school at 15 or 16 years of age, the Regulations require a stated amount for the child. But as they are not, as a rule, competent to expend this wage wisely and well, we expect it to be spent under the teaching and direction of the master or mistress, as a part of the childs training. And another part of this training is *saving*. We believe that in most cases the whole wage in not necessary each year for clothing, pocket money etc. If near a bank a savings account should be started. If not the money can be sent to the manager by postal note to be deposited in bank in the childs name. *An account is required to be kept* is of how the wage has been expended in order to satisfy the Inspector that the Regulation has been observed. He also consults the School Register for the facts regarding school attendance. If a child is taken when young and has grown up as one of the family and has been well provided for to the satisfaction of the Inspector the provisions regarding "wages" may be relaxed. In case of removal, in practice, we do not require, except in serious cases that the child be sent to the Home at Halifax but to save the employer and ourselves expense we have it sent to some other home in the same or an adjoining county. *Notice should be given* the Home of severe illness, death, change of the family address, marriage or any serious trouble. We favor homes with very few or no young children, homes near schools and in the country and small villages rather than in the towns and cities. We require the master and mistress from the beginning to enforce obedience, carefulness, promptness, good manners, truthfulness, honesty etc. Anyone who does not intend to make these children do as they ought even to using various more or less severe punishments ought not to get them and if one out of a score turns out badly do not judge all the children by that one but look up the records of the other nineteen.

The Middlemore Home

FAIRVIEW STATION, : : HALIFAX, N. S.

J. STERLING KING, Manager

Application for Boy

Kindly fill in this form and return at once to above address

I hereby apply for a boy of _____ years, and, if successful in my application, I agree to provide him proper food and clothing, so that he shall be as well clothed as at present, and medical attendance; also with such Common School Education as is supplied in the District where I reside for at least 5 months of each year; and I undertake that he shall attend Sunday School and Divine Worship. I further undertake when he is 16 years old to pay him instead of providing clothing and schooling $5.00 per month for services he may render me and also to retain him in my employ up to the age of 18 years, unless there be full and adequate cause for his removal; in which case he must be returned to the Middlemore Home after not less than a month's notice with as good a supply of clothes as when I received him, and not be placed in another home without first obtaining consent of the manager of the Middlemore Home. I agree to keep an account showing price of all kinds of clothing, shoes, etc. necessary summer or winter, for Sunday or for work, and pocket money to the amount of above wages, except whenever reasonably well supplied with clothing, the wages or any part, is deposited in Savings Bank or with the Home Manager, for the boy's future use. I agree to furnish a report as often as required of his (1) health, (2) general conduct, (3) education and (4) wages received. I acknowledge the Home Manager to be the Guardian of the said boy, and I agree to permit him or his agents, at all times to have access to the said boy and I acknowledge the right of the Home Manager or his agent to remove him from my custody if he shall consider it in the interest of said boy to do so, with not less than as good a supply of clothing as when I received him.

Signature *Neil D. McInnis*

Address *Glenville, Inverness Co., N.S.*

Witness *Henry Meeling* Date *Jan 11/15*

KINDLY ANSWER THE FOLLOWING QUESTIONS:—

Are you married? _____ If not, who is Housekeeper? _____

Give age and sex of any children at your home? _____

Is there Consumption or any contagious disease in your home? _____

How far do you reside from your Church? _____ From School? _____

And from nearest Railway Station? _____ Give name of Station? _____

Is the School open during the Winter Months? _____

Give Name and Address of the Pastor of the Church you attend _____

One other reference _____

Joe Payne
1st June 1915.

10 years Sept 11/15.

Contents

1	Joe Payne 1914	1
2	Alice Payne 1914	5
3	Christy MacInnis 1914	19
4	Middlemore Emigration Home 1914	25
5	Canada 1915	35
6	Glenville, Cape Breton 1915 - 1924	41
7	Finding Work 1924 - 1932	95
8	Ola, Truro, Nova Scotia 1932 - 1945	119
9	Carolyn 1945	137
Epilogue	Celebrations and Apology	155
Acknowledgements		166

All Alone Again
Joe Payne, British Home Child

Chapter 1

<u>Joe Payne</u>
<u>Birmingham, England (September 1914)</u>

    Joe, without a backward glance at his mum, bounced down the steps. He was glad to escape the heat and stench inside the tiny room they lived in. He skipped across the courtyard, past the one water tap the eight families shared. He called as he went, to his friend Eddie, sitting on his stoop.
    Joe was extremely small for his age with large brown prominent eyes in a rather flat face. Both boys were nine years old.

They were ill-nourished children, with straggly, greasy hair the color of mud. Their clothes, though clean, were threadbare and barely fit their skinny bodies. Normally, every morning, the boys escaped their tiny lodgings as early as possible and spent the day together, running through the streets of Birmingham.

Birmingham, built along the River Rea by the Anglo Saxons in the 7th century, had become a city in 1889. By 1914, it was the second largest city in England, second only to London in population. Industries, which created noise, smoke and pollution had created a large oppressed population of working-class people.

Joe lived with his mum and baby sister in a combined room in a row of small terraced houses that ran the whole length of the street. These back to back units were two or three stories high, with one room per floor. They had been built in the 1800's, to accommodate the fast-growing, overpopulated city. They were in a typical, big city, working-class area, which included shops and pubs on the corners of the streets. There was a communal wash house, which consisted of a row of metal tubs set in brickwork, under which a fire was lit to boil water for washing clothes. Clotheslines crisscrossed the yard.

The outside toilets, back to back between properties, had to be emptied into a horse-drawn tanker every so often. That job was usually done at night. With only one water pipe, drinking water came from an outside tap. The drainage was poor and often there was flooding. No one knew at the time that dirty water carried the deadly cholera bacteria.

Joe's mum and the other women worked hard dealing with heat and poor sanitation. They kept everything as neat and clean as possible. They had to contend with the whole family living together in a small, dark room, infested with lice, fleas and bedbugs. It was nothing to see a mouse or rat scurry across the floor. Although the rich considered this type of housing a slum area; having a job, a wage and a roof over your head, were the three most important things to a poor family. They were all in the same boat and made the best out of a bad situation.

On that particular day, Eddie didn't move off the step. He just sat there spinning his wooden peg-top, a toy his father had carved.

"Are you coming"? Joe asked.

All Alone Again
Joe Payne, British Home Child

"Can't!" Eddie replied. "Foot too sore. I can't walk." Eddie held up his injured foot as proof. "See, when we were digging around at the dump yesterday, a piece of glass went through the hole in my boots."

The boots Eddie had worn were passed down from his older brother, Dan. The large holes in the soles could not protect him from the shard of broken glass.

"Go on without me," Eddie continued. "Watch out for those Burtley lads though. You don't want to get your arm twisted again."

The hungry children who didn't have jobs, ran wildly through the streets, pilfering when they saw anything they could find, a pocket knife or perhaps a bun to keep them from starving. Some of the bigger boys could be quite troublesome to the younger, smaller boys. The Burtley lads were a large gang of brothers and cousins aged five to fifteen who because of poverty were forced into a life of crime.

Eddie wasn't sitting on the step the next morning. When Joe and his mum were eating supper that night, Joe's mother mentioned that Eddie had a fever.

The following day Joe knocked on Eddie's cottage door. Meg, Eddie's sister, said her brother was still sick. Evidently, there was poison in the foot that had spread into his blood. Most often, poor families could not afford a doctor. Eddie's dad got some tonic at the drugstore that was supposed to cure anything and everything. They hoped against hope that the tonic would work, and that Eddie would soon be well again.

The tonic didn't cure Eddie and a few days later, when the doctor was finally called, there was nothing he could do. There was no such thing as penicillin in the early 1900's and it was too late to amputate the foot as gangrene had already set in. Eddie's whole body was septic. Before Joe knew it, Eddie was gone and buried just like so many other children. It seemed, every winter, there was some plague that went through the city taking some of the parents and half of the babies and young children. Death in childhood was common! Death and disease were often caused by heat and poor sanitation among those who also lacked proper nutrition and hygiene.

Thus far, Joe had survived! He was a happy lad. He didn't have much and he didn't expect much. It was the life he knew. He guessed he fared as well as the others. He hadn't seen his dad in a long time, but he had his mum and his sister, and they had a roof over their heads, even if they were crowded into a filthy slum.

Joe was used to seeing death every day. He missed the Clinton children. His mum had been a housekeeper for the widowed Mr. Clinton last year. He knew the whole Clinton family had been sick. His mum never told him they had died, but he suspected it, even though he didn't ask. Joe had moved so often. Just last month, he had moved to this new home.

But now, sitting on his stoop alone, he missed Eddie. Joe looked across at Eddie's vacant step and pushed his fists tight into both eyes to keep from crying. He was the man of the house now, and he was expected to be strong.

Chapter 2

<u>Alice Payne
Birmingham, England (September 1914)</u>

Alice moved to close the outside door that her son had left ajar. She paused in the doorway for a moment thinking to take in a breath of fresh air. The one room she lived in with her two children was very hot. The stench outside, however, was terrible. And flies! They would drive a body mad.

Her poor boy, she thought as she watched Joe skip across the courtyard. What would happen to him? What would become of all of them, but especially Joe?

Life wasn't easy for the common people in the early 1900's. There was an enormous gap between the rich and the poor. The poor lived in overcrowded conditions where the survival rate was low. Massive industrialization had brought too many people into the cities. The earnings, if any, were very little, and people lived hand to mouth. The workhouses held ten times the women and children they were meant to house.

Alice had been a seventh child born to Thomas and Ruth Sturch in 1883. Her father had been a boot maker but could not support his family of nine. When Alice was five years old, Sarah Gardner, her father's sister, offered to raise Alice. Sarah, her husband George who was a publican and their daughter Winnifred lived in Bath Cottage, in Blockley, in the North Cotswolds of England. Blockley was well known for its numerous water mills, used for the wool trade. Water turbines had been installed giving Blockley the first regular, electricity supply in the country. Bath Cottage was one of nearly one hundred, separate properties on the estate of Northwick Park. It was so named because it had, what was thought to be the remains of Roman baths, in the garden that actually faced one of the old water mills.

George and Sarah Gardner

In March of 1889, it was the Gardners who had Alice baptized. When Sarah died, Alice remained living in the Gardner household, until she was nineteen.

Alice's father's watch

All Alone Again
Joe Payne, British Home Child

When Alice was in her late teens, she would often work at Northwick House. In medieval times, Northwick had been a settlement of smallholders. Surrounding the mansion had been small farms let out for cultivation. In the 16th century it had been owned by the Spencer family, ancestors of Diana, Princess of Wales. The mansion was magnificent. It was three stories high with tall bay windows. The entrance hall was grand. Four ranges of rooms surrounded a central staircase. There was a huge picture gallery, built by the second Lord Northwick, an avid art collector. The mansion had more than one kitchen and a fine cellar for storing food. Close by, there were servant quarters, stables and a coach house with a front covered in finely carved stonework. The mansion provided work for butlers, footmen, cooks, maids, and a housekeeper, as well as outside staff. The property included a lake, park land, and farms.

The third Lord Northwick had died in 1887 leaving no surviving children. It was Lady Northwick's family from a previous marriage who would inherit Northwick.

There were sometimes grand occasions at the mansion. Everything would be cleaned and polished while the cooks were busy in the kitchen preparing all kinds of delicacies. Alice remembered one special occasion when Lady Northwick's grandson, George Spencer Churchill, came for a visit and brought with him his cousin, Winston Churchill. The cousins were close and only a few years older than Alice. Alice and the other maids would go out of their way to catch a glimpse of the visiting gentlemen.

In 1912, George would inherit Lady Northwick's castle while his cousin would later become Sir Winston Leonard Spencer-Churchill, Prime Minister of the United Kingdom in 1940.

It wasn't all work at the mansion. On an afternoon or evening off, Alice would often go to the local pub with some of the other servant girls. It was there, in 1902, that she caught the eye of the handsome Josiah Payne. He was tall, dark and incredibly interesting. Josiah, at the age of twenty-seven, had just come back from South Africa, after serving in the second Boer war with Britain. The war, from 1889 to 1902, saw Britain in conflict with the Boers. The Boers were descendants of the Dutch settlers in South Africa, who had wanted their independence. The conflict between the British army

Carolyn MacIsaac

and the Dutch settlers had led to war. Josiah had received a medal from the King's Royal Rifle Corp which he wore proudly.

Josiah's medal

Josiah in the middle, top row, with his family

Alice

All Alone Again
Joe Payne, British Home Child

Alice

Alice and Josiah

    In 1902, Alice and Josiah were married at the age of nineteen and twenty-seven. They made a handsome couple. Alice, although tall, looked short beside Josiah. She wore her long softly curled light brown hair in an updo. Queen Victoria had died in January 1901, and King Edward V11 presently sat on the throne. In the new Edwardian era women wore picture hats. Lady Northwick's lady's maid had lent Alice a gold hat that matched the long brown dress she wore on special occasions. Lady Northwick gave the newlyweds a china teapot with a picture of Northwick on it as a wedding gift. It was number 32 in a limited edition.

On September 11, 1905, while Josiah drank at the local pub, where he and Alice had initially met three years earlier, a midwife was called to their home. After many hours of hard labor, Alice delivered a son, to carry on his father's name. They had him baptized Joseph Payne on October 29, 1905, in the Church of England, in Gloucestershire. He wasn't given a middle name. Middle names were not the norm for the lower class.

Sometimes, Josiah would disappear for days or even weeks, often having to travel away from home to find work as a farm laborer. Times were hard but most likely Josiah had returned from the war, with scars on the inside where no one could see them, in what today would be diagnosed and treated as Post-Traumatic Stress Disorder or PTSD. In the early 1900's, it was known as shell shock.

In May of 1910, King Edward VII died at the age of sixty-eight. He had only reigned nine years. The crown was passed on to his second son who became King George 5th. Joe and the other school children were given a cup with a picture of the new king on it.

Alice also left their home at Brooklane cottages, in Blockley and moved to Murcot, North Childwickham, where she found work in the strawberry fields or worked with other seasonal crops. While she lived in Murcot, Alice gave birth to her second child on June 19, 1910. The baby was baptized, Georgina Maud Payne. Joe nicknamed his baby sister Ena.

All Alone Again
Joe Payne, British Home Child

Strawberry Picking

Alice and Ena

Josiah was always getting into some kind of trouble. From time to time he was caught poaching or some other offence. When Joe was four and Georgina still a baby, due to his heavy drinking, Josiah lost his job as a cowman. Alice got a separation order listing his heavy drinking and his leaving her for weeks at a time as the reason.

Having no way to survive on her own, she took a job housekeeping for George Clinton. George's wife had died leaving him with three children, eight, ten, and eleven years old, to raise alone.

In 1911, the typhoid epidemic caught George. He was only 46 years old. The life expectancy at that time was only age 47 for men and age 50 for women. Alice wasn't sure what happened to his children. She had two of her own to worry about.

***

Three of Josiah's brothers migrated to Canada the same year and settled in Alberta, one of Canada's three Prairie Provinces. Canada, a self-governing dominion of the British Empire, was a young country with mostly forests and large lakes. It bordered on both the Atlantic and Pacific Ocean. Although thirty-six times as large as the United Kingdom, the population in the United Kingdom was eight times what the population of Canada was. The brothers gave up everything for the dream that there would be a chance for a better life in Canada.

Josiah thought of going to Canada with his brothers, but he realized he had responsibilities in England, and for a time, he and Alice got back together. They lived in Murcot until his drinking habits once more became too much for her. In 1914, Josiah returned to the army and fought with the East Kent Regiment (the Buffs) throughout the First World War. During the war, Alice had no contact with Josiah. When a soldier was at war, his family never knew where he was, or even if he was alive. In those days there was no social welfare, or any other help for widows and unwed mothers, or for women whose husbands were away to war. There were only poorhouses, or workhouses, for people in her state. Alice didn't know that she would never see Josiah again.

It was a last resort, but when the seasonal work was finished in Murcot, in 1914, with her husband gone, and no income to provide food for her children, the desperate Alice packed up her meager belongings and along with her two children took a train to the city of Birmingham. Birmingham was known as a city of a thousand trades. It was a world leader in the production of pens, buckles, buttons, jewelry and guns. Alice was only one of about 200,000 people who moved to the center of Birmingham to find work. She made the best

All Alone Again
Joe Payne, British Home Child

of a bad situation. Like everyone else, when she moved from the little village of Murcot to the large city of Birmingham, she had to adapt. Through help from the church, she was able to find a place for them to live in Saint Martin's Place. Even though the thousands of slum areas had been demolished, they were not replaced with better housing, but rather with new streets, railways and businesses. Almost no provision had been made for the people who had lost their homes when they were torn down, not to mention the thousands moving into the area. The new housing was inadequate to house the thousands of displaced poor. Alice had brought furniture and little things to brighter up their home with her, but the combined room Alice and the children moved into was gloomy and unsanitary, and Alice still considered it a slum.

Alice quickly got a job in a factory making metal parts for prams. With men leaving their jobs when they went to fight in the war, large numbers of women were recruited into the vacated jobs. The earnings were low, but she made enough to put some food on the table.

Alice made arrangements with a neighbour to look after four year old Georgina while she was at work, but when Joe wasn't in school, he was on his own. Alice had to be on the job by 5:30 in the morning and worked a twelve hour day.

On payday, on her way home from work, Alice might stop at the Butcher shop for a small piece of mutton to cook for their supper. Many nights there would be just vegetables without the meat. Some of the food shops had recently closed after they were emptied by anxious shoppers. Although food was not rationed as yet, voluntary restraint was suggested because with the country at war some food might not be available. Many people panicked. They were afraid of a food shortage because Britain relied heavily on food from abroad. 80% of wheat, 40% of meat and almost all sugar was imported. People bought and stored what they could afford. The poor, unable to buy ahead, faced a shortage of food.

Sunday morning, although she felt like staying in bed all day, Alice got herself and the children ready for church. She wore her long grey dress, the bottom brushed to remove any dust it had acquired while dragging on the dusty ground. The Sunday dress was not washed very often. She wore an apron over it and would remove the dress and hang it back up as soon as she got home from church.

It was a warm September day and the sun was shining. Joe wore short pants that were so loose and baggy they came to the top of his boots. Georgina's long, curly blond hair was tied off her face with a large pink bow. She wore a light cotton dress and boots much like her mother's. Alice threw a shawl she had knit over her shoulders as they left the house.

The three of them enjoyed the walk on a warm sunny day. There had been no air raids on the city as yet, and for once the smog wasn't too bad. Even four year old Georgina didn't find the walk to Saint Martin's Cathedral too long. She was just glad to be spending the day with her mother.

Saint Martin's, a parish church of the Church of England was situated in The Bull Ring, a major commercial area that had been in the center of Birmingham since the Middle Ages. Other than the preservation of the tower and spire, the church had been demolished and rebuilt in 1873. Its exterior was made with Grimshill stone and the interior of sandstone. It had an open hammer beam roof the same as Westminster Hall. During the demolition, painted beams had been found behind the plaster ceiling. Medieval wall paintings and decorations were also found in the chancel.

Tears welled in Alice's eyes when they sang the old hymn "Just a Closer walk With Thee…I am weak but thou art strong". She feared she had no strength left in her. She could only go on by believing the Lord was with her. For the rest of her life, this particular hymn was linked to some precious memory and would make her cry.

A wide area fronting Saint Martin's church formed the marketplace. There were over 600 market stalls, selling anything from flowers to fish. After the church service Alice wandered around the market with the children, enjoying the afternoon. She stopped at a vender and bought them each a bun. They passed the rings where horses used to be traded and bulls were baited before slaughter. They stopped beside a Lord Nelson statue and listened to a Holy Joe preacher warn people that their sinful nature was leading them to hell unless they repented and accepted Jesus Christ as their Saviour.

Alice stopped to sit on a bench and rest her tired aching feet. Joe chased after Georgina as she ran from one thing to another with a

All Alone Again
Joe Payne, British Home Child

child's endless energy. A woman with a little girl and three young boys came and sat beside her and introduced herself as Margaret. It turned out that they were close neighbours.

Georgina, curious to see who her mother was speaking with, ran up and stood looking at the newcomers. Joe followed and soon was off playing with the boys.

When it was discovered they lived in the same row of houses, they all walked home together. Joe promised Eddie that he would pick him up for school the next day.

As they left the market, they passed through a wide entrance with two grand Doric columns on either side. A large metal gate would be pulled across at the end of the day. With gas lighting in the market, even in winter the market could be kept open until late in the evening.

Joe and Eddie were both in grade three and soon became fast friends. Joe, on his own after school, until his mother returned from work in the evening, would spend the remainder of the day with Eddie and sometimes Eddie's brothers, Dan and Frank. One day Eddie found some fish hooks and a bit of line. The two boys snuck off by themselves and headed down to the River Ria. They cut two small branches off an alder bush, tied the line to it and fastened a fish hook on the end. They dug at the edge of the river with a stick looking for worms.

As they sat on the edge of the river, holding a fishing pole with the line dangling in the water, a couple of boys approached them, snickering to each other. "What ya hoping to catch? There ain't no fish in this river. If you want to catch fish, you'll have to go to the canals. But say, when you were digging for worms, did you come across any old knives or anything"? One of the boys proceeded to tell Joe and Eddie that Stone Age hunters had roamed around the River Ria Valley ten thousand years earlier. Pieces of their hunting knives had been found right were the boys had dug for worms. The archeologists had also found gold and silver belonging to the Anglo Saxons dating back to the 7th century.

The boys were right. They didn't catch any fish but they had fun on their adventure and it was perhaps more educational than anything they had learned in the overcrowded classroom that day.

Joe discovered the boys names were Robert and Charley Burtley. They told Joe and Eddie that the only place to go fishing was in the canals. If Eddie and Joe would provide the hooks they would take them there on Saturday. "Meet us by the entrance to the Bull Ring at eight." Then with a nod they were off, and it was time for Joe and Eddie to return home.

Saturday morning Joe and Eddie hung around the entrance to the Bull Ring for almost an hour. A suffragette parade marched by, made up of women holding signs wanting the right to vote.

Joe and Eddie were almost ready to give up when a group of bigger boys came along pulling an old cart. Robert and Charley were among them. "Change of plans," Charley said. "This is the rest of the Burtley boys, and we have a job to do. It's down in the canals so you can tag along if you like."

The boys said no more and as they walked away Joe and Eddie followed. One of the older boys pushed against Eddie and made fun of his handmade fishing rod. Another older brother turned and sneered at Eddie. Joe and Eddie were both a little nervous around the bigger boy's rough housing, but they wanted to see these canals where they might find fish.

"So, if we aren't going to fish, what are we going to do?" Joe asked quietly of Charley. Charley was probably the youngest of the boys, but still larger than Joe or Eddie.

"We swim," he answered, cautiously looking to his older brothers.

"I can't swim," Joe stated. "How deep is the water?"

"You can watch," Charley nodded, feeling sure of himself. "And you can help us carry the coal back."

It turned out Charley and Robert and their mates swam in the canal quite often, especially by the low bridges and tunnels. Over 170 miles of connecting canals had been built in the 18th and 19th century. There were thirty-five miles of canals in Birmingham alone. Raw materials were brought into the city through them and finished goods sent back out. In 1914, the canals were busy waterways transporting coal, iron and other heavy goods.

The boys would dive down to the bottom of the water and bring out the coal that had been knocked off the barges that were overloaded and take it home on the old cart. They became quiet as they approached a bridge. The area was bustling with activity. More than once they had been chased by the local bobby (policeman).

At one point, when one of the older boys was running up the bank, Joe must have been in his way for he grabbed Joe's arm as if it were a branch on a tree and shoved him out of his way. While the Burtley boys were busy in the water, Joe and Eddie snuck away with their fishing rods. They tried to avoid the Burtley lads after that, and someone at school mentioned the two oldest boys had landed in jail for stealing.

***

September 1914, Alice found herself in a position where she could not keep going on her own. Her job had been suspended due to the war. Bit by bit she had sold her furniture to buy food and pay rent. Even her wedding ring had been pawned to buy food. Behind in her rent, exhausted from the long hours she had been working and having to deal with her living conditions, she was also sick. The doctor said she needed to go in the hospital for an operation, a hysterectomy, he said.

Joe had been getting into a lot of trouble with the police. It was mostly small things like food that he was stealing. Inspector Chadwick was worried about the small boy. He had spoken to Alice on several occasions and told her that she needed to put Joe in an orphanage. Joe was one of the thousands of destitute children to be placed in a home because their parents were either dead or too ill to care for them.

Unlike the early 1800's, where children had been a means to an income, now a century later there were those who wanted a better life for the children. Such a man was John Middlemore. He had opened a children's home in Birmingham forty years earlier to take in starving and disadvantaged children like Joe. Mr. Middlemore was a kind, sensitive man who loved children and devoted his life to helping them. It was there, at Middlemore Emigration Home, the inspector sent Alice. Joe would go there to live. Somehow, Alice would be able to keep Ena with her.

Alice also had to consider that England was at war. The previous month on August 4, 1914, England had entered the war against Germany. The Germans had started the war by invading and now occupying Belgium. England would not be a safe place for children running wild in the streets.

As Alice stood in the doorway, watching Joe talking to his playmate Eddie, she realized the inspector was right. He had to be right. England was no place for a young boy like Joe. A slight wind could blow him over. He probably weighed less than his three-year-old sister, and Joe had just turned nine. He might not survive another winter. He would be put in Middlemore, a home for destitute children like himself. There he would be bathed and clothed and fed properly. Perhaps he would finally get a bit of fat on those skinny bones of his. It would tear her heart out, but it needed to be done, and it would be best for Joe. It wouldn't be long until she was well and on her feet again. The war would be over, and he would come home.

Unless...Canada... There was talk that Middlemore homes, along with some other homes in England, were sending homeless children across the sea to Canada. It seemed that England had too many children, and Canada... Well, it was a young country. There were farms there, with big, open, grassy fields with cows and horses and other animals. Alice was told that some of the farmers there were willing to rescue poor English orphans and give them a home. What a life Joe would have! Off the streets in England! Away from all the trouble, he could get into! She could picture him running across a field with a full belly and laughing, as Joe loved to laugh, even when there was nothing she could see to laugh about. Alice could picture Joe running through an apple orchard. She could picture him reaching up and picking an apple off a tree and happily munching on it. There would probably be a dog running with him. If Joe missed his family, which he surely would, the dog might be his best friend. The dog would mend Joe's broken heart.

Yes, she had a decision to make but then there really was no decision. Middlemore was the obvious choice. As much as it would hurt her to give Joe up, it had to be the best thing for him. Others were in a position to give Joe what she couldn't.

Chapter 3

Christy MacInnis
Glenville, Nova Scotia (September 1914)

As Alice stood in her doorway in Birmingham England, across the sea, in the small village of Glenville, on Cape Breton Island, stood another burdened mother watching her boy. Both weary mothers were wondering what would become of their sons and how the boys would survive life's hardships.

It was ten o'clock in the morning, in Birmingham, but only five o'clock on Cape Breton Island.

Neil, who was barely twenty, had a lot of responsibility. He was the only boy in a family of eight. The fatherless young man had to help provide for, a mother, and five younger sisters. An older sister, Mary Sarah, was married and living in Truro, on the mainland of Nova Scotia. His sisters, Mary Christine, Christy, Jessie, Hughena and Alena, still lived at home. Their ages ranged from six to seventeen. Cape Bretoners often named their children after the Mother Mary or gave them other Christian names. Thus, Christy MacInnis had a sister Christy Ann. Her daughters were Mary Sarah, Mary Christine, Christine, Jessie, Hughena and Alena. The repetition was often confusing.

It was not yet daylight, and Neil was heading out, lantern in hand, to bring the cows in from the pasture for milking. Then he would clean the manure out of the gutter and head the animals back out to pasture. Mary, four years younger than Neil, was upstairs getting dressed and would join him shortly. Still half asleep, Mary pulled a white slip and brown dress on over her head. She quickly parted her long brown hair in the middle and braided it into two braids, one on each side of her head. She struggled with the black stockings before putting on her black boots. Mary had barn chores to do before she left for school with her younger sisters.

Besides cows, the family raised sheep, pigs, and chickens and kept four workhorses. In the summer months, the animals grazed on grass and could be left in the field all night. As the nights got colder, the animals had to be brought back to the barn before supper. The girls would help herd the animals back inside for milking, after they put down clean straw for them to lie on.

Come winter, the animals would have to be fed inside. The MacInnis family grew their own oats and corn to feed the animals. The grass in the fields was cut twice during the summer. The whole family worked to pile it high on the wagon, then filled the hayloft in the barn.

The cows, sheep and horses would be fed hay, along with some oats or grain. The pigs also had to be fed again in the evening. If they were overfed in the morning, they would only eat part of their food and destroy the remainder playing and walking in it. Pigs were also given the scraps of food from the table, vegetable peelings, plus extra cut up potatoes, turnip, corn and apples. Some grain was mixed into their slop. Pigs do not digest hay very well. The chickens, who picked away at seeds and bugs on the ground each day, were also fed scraps of food.

Christy MacInnis, called Ma by her children, was inside preparing breakfast. The kitchen was a large room, where the family, when not busy with chores, spent most of their time. On the inside

All Alone Again
Joe Payne, British Home Child

wall was a wood cook stove with an attached water tank for heating water. The stove was the only means of heating the house. On the wall across from the stove was a washstand with a basin for pouring water to wash their hands. A long black horsehair lounge was under the window. Neil would rest here when the evening chores were done, just as his father had done when he was alive.

Christy was making a large pot of oatmeal porridge. Neil and Mary would be hungry when they came back inside for breakfast. When she heard them coming, she would break some eggs into the frying pan she had placed towards the back of the stove to keep warm. Bread, baked the day before, was already sliced and placed beside the butter she had churned, on the large square table in front of the window. There was a pitcher of cream, skimmed off the top of the unpasteurized milk, to pour over the porridge. By the time breakfast was ready the other girls would be up. Hughena and Alena would help feed the chickens, while Jessie and Christy cleared the table and did the dishes before they got ready for school.

The girls had at least a mile walk to the little white, one-room school house down the road. When Neil had attended the school, he often went early, to start a fire in the wood stove, which was the means of heating the small building. The boys would take turns, going early, one week at a time, to start the fire. Now that Neil's schooling was finished, other boys had that job. The school would be fairly warm, by the time the teacher and her other students arrived. It wouldn't take much to warm the building this time of year, as the afternoons were still fairly warm but by January they would be very thankful for the heat to warm their frozen fingers and toes. The wood stove was situated in the middle of the room. On an extremely cold day in January, the teacher would practically sit on top of the stove. The children always said she was hogging all the heat.

While the girls attended school, Christy separated the milk Neil had collected and washed the eggs the girls had gathered. This morning she would churn butter. The milk was kept in pails and hung in the well to keep cool. There would be enough milk collected in a week, as well as several dozen eggs, to trade in return for the flour and sugar she needed. She would harness the horses to the buggy and drive to Inverness, later that day, for the exchange.

Christy also hoped to get some bolts of fabric. The girls were outgrowing their clothes quickly. The ones passed down to them were becoming more and more threadbare, as each sister acquired an older sister's dress she had outgrown. She would do her best to sew the older girls a new dress for Christmas.

Before she harnessed up the horse to the buggy, Christy wanted to finish making a batch of apple jelly. The girls had picked apples off the trees in the orchard the day before. They had cooked them on the stove last evening. Before she went to bed, Christy had poured the mushy apples into a clean cloth bag, she had made. She tied a string around the top of the bag and hung it from a beam in the pantry ceiling, so that the clear fluid would drip all night, into a large pot sitting beneath it.

Mary had dug out a dozen bottles and washed them last evening. Christy would boil water this morning and pour it into the jars to sterilize them, just before she poured the hot sweetened liquid into them. She had added a cup of white sugar for every cup of juice and hoped there was enough pectin in the apples to set it.

It was getting hot in the kitchen. Christy had to keep adding wood to the fire to keep the liquid gently rolling but not so much that it would boil hard. After about an hour, she took a spoonful and set it aside to see if it jelled. When she was satisfied, she quickly sterilized the jars and covers. She then poured the hot liquid into the bottles and quickly screwed the tops on.

Christy stood back and admired the dozen red jars of apple jelly that the girls would put away in the pantry cupboard, along with the blackberry, strawberry and raspberry jams they had helped her make earlier in the season. The shelves were full now. Besides jams and jelly, there were pickled beets and tomato chow and cucumber pickles, to add to their dinners the coming winter.

The cucumbers and tomatoes were pretty well done in the garden, but there were potatoes and carrots and turnips to dig yet and store in the cold cellar. The girls would have to help with that after school and on Saturdays. Perhaps a couple of the older girls would have to stay home from school a few days. Neil and Christy wouldn't have time to get to it all. Neil also had to plow the soil in the garden after all the vegetables were removed.

All Alone Again
Joe Payne, British Home Child

Plowing, planting and feeding animals along with raising seven children; was far more work than was possible. Every night Christy crawled into her bed exhausted.

Christy had lost her dear, husband, Allan, to pneumonia last winter and now her son Neil and her daughters were barely managing. Christy did not allow herself to think what would happen if Neil had to go to war. Because Canada was part of the British Commonwealth, when Britain declared war on Germany, Canada was automatically at war with them as well.

Much of Cape Breton was Catholic, but the MacInnis family attended the Protestant Presbyterian Church in Strathlorn. Sunday morning, the family rose early to get the chores done, before they got dressed in their finest clothes. Then they hitched the wagon to the horses and drove to church.

After the service was a time of visiting. Sometimes one or two of the girls would be invited to someone's home for dinner. Sometimes Christy would have them invite a friend over to their home. Sunday dinner was usually a chicken or a roast of pork or beef, from one of their own animals they had slaughtered. Especially this time of year, vegetables were plentiful. Potatoes, carrots, turnip, cabbage and parsnip would surround the roast cooked in the oven with a little onion added for flavor. For this meal, the family would sit at the long table in the dining room, situated off the kitchen. If they had company, Ma and the older children might sit in the seldom-used parlor after the meal was finished, while the younger girls did the dishes.

On this particular day, in late September, Mary MacDonald stopped to ask Christy how she was doing and asked her if she had ever considered getting a Home Child to help around the farm. Christy had never heard of a Home Child. Mary told her about a family she knew who lived just outside Inverness. The mother of four young children had fallen off a horse the previous year. With damage to her spine, she could barely get out of bed. The government provided help for her by arranging to have a girl brought over from England to do the work she could no longer do.

Christy told Mary she had never heard of a Home Child. She didn't think she could have a stranger in her home, but she did ponder the thought. What if they could get a strong teenage boy to help Neil? She would ask Mary more about it next Sunday.

Before they got back to church the following Sunday, Christy met up with Mary MacDonald in Inverness. Christy had been taking more butter and eggs to town.

"I'd like to ask you more about the girl from England" Christy spoke in Gaelic, the Scottish dialect.

"Are you thinking of it then, Christy?" Mary replied, also in Gaelic.

"I cannot imagine taking a stranger into our home. I have five young ladies to think of, but it could possibly be an answer to prayer. I want to know more about it before I mention it to Neil."

"Like I told you, this lady was in a bad way, not able to get out of bed and her with four children under the age of seven. Somebody tells her husband, about these forms to fill out, to get a child from England. I believe the girl is about thirteen or fourteen and is very capable of doing the cleaning and making of meals and helping with the children. Mrs. MacLean said it was a godsend."

"Why are these older children coming from England?"

"England is in a bad state, so it is. There is much poverty in the overcrowded cities and not enough food. Children are literally taken off the streets and put in a big home, where they are cleaned up and taught how to do domestic work or some sort of trade or farm work. England and Canada have partnered up for us to take the children to Canada and feed them. In return for a good day's work, the children earn room and board."

"How old are these children? I would need a boy, one practically a man, good and strong, to help Neil. Girls, I have enough of."

"I believe the MacLean's had to sign a paper saying they would keep the girl until she was eighteen but someone else said they knew of a family who had taken in a three-year-old girl. What good she would be, I don't know, but perhaps they think they can train her from a young age."

Chapter 4

Middlemore Emigration Home
Birmingham, England (October 1914)

It was mid-October, 1914 when Joe arrived home one afternoon to find a well-dressed gentleman sitting at the table with his mum. The man looked uncomfortable. Alice's face was smeared with tear stains.

Joe looked from one to the other with apprehension!

Alice couldn't get any words out. It was the man who told Joe he would be taking him away for a while. He told Joe about a big house, where many boys and girls lived when their parents were not able to look after them.

Joe looked at his Mother. "Mum?" he said questioningly.

Alice took a deep breath. She had to hold it together. "Joe," she replied quietly, "this man will give you a good home until I am well again."

Joe had seen too much sickness and death. "Are you dying?" He struggled to get the words out.

"No Joe, don't get upset. I need to have an operation, but I will get better. You go with this kind man for now; they will feed you and give you a bed to sleep in until I am well. It won't be for very long."

"What about Ena?"

"They will allow her to stay with me because she is still a baby. The home only takes children between the ages of seven and fourteen." Alice sighed. "Joe, be strong now, you are a big boy, nine years old. Be good, and do what they tell you. And don't cry!"

Alice held her boy tightly to her for a long minute, before the man took Joe's hand and led him out the door to the waiting buggy. Joe took nothing with him. He would be bathed immediately when he reached the home. His head would be shaved and scrubbed with something to get rid of any lice he might have. The clothes he wore would be burnt, and he would be given a clean shirt and pants to wear.

Middlemore Emigration Home was a large three-story brick building on Saint Luke's Road, in Birmingham, England. It had been founded by John Middlemore forty years before. Mr. Middlemore was a kind man who wanted to help children who were victims of inescapable poverty. Besides teaching the children a trade, he, more importantly, taught them self-respect, good habits and cleanliness. He didn't want the children to feel ashamed or have a stigma attached to them.

The home was in an area of Birmingham Joe had never seen before. He looked up at all the rows of tall, narrow windows. He stumbled, he was shaking so badly, as he walked up the steps. The gentleman with him opened the door, and inside, along the long halls ahead, Joe saw children of different ages scurrying in many directions. None of them paid Joe and the man any attention.

They entered a large office, where an older woman, sitting at a desk, asked Joe several questions.

All Alone Again
Joe Payne, British Home Child

"What is your full name?"

"Joseph Payne."

"Your middle name as well please."

"I don't have one."

"Everyone has a middle name." She mumbled, "I've heard this from too many children. It's like their parents couldn't be bothered to name them properly." She went on to the next question. "What is your mother's address?"

My address too, Joe thought, as he answered "Six Saint Martin's Drive, Birmingham, England." Joe thought, rightly so, that it might be important to remember that address.

When the necessary papers were filled out, a matron arrived and took Joe upstairs. He was taken to a storage room filled with clothes. The matron pulled a shirt and a pair of pants off the shelf and held them up in front of Joe. "This will do," she muttered to herself more than to Joe. She added underwear, socks, a vest, a tie and boots, to the pile in her arms and said to Joe, "Come along now".

Joe stared at her but followed. He was speechless. Were these new clothes for him? He had never had new clothes before and never had clothes that fit, ever.

The next room they entered was a large bathroom. There were several toilets and bathtubs. Joe's scalp, after it had been shaved, was washed with some really stinky stuff that burned. His whole body was scrubbed with a black soap until his skin felt raw.

By the time Joe was clean and dressed, he was completely in a trance. What was happening to him? He would try to be a brave boy so that his mum would be proud, but how he wished she would get better quickly and he could go back home.

"There, there now," the matron said with a smile. "Don't you look nice! Let's go back to the storage room and get you some more clothes so that you will have a change and a coat, hat and mittens to wear on cold days. There is a storage box at the end of your bed in which to keep all your belongings."

After the new items were chosen, along with a toothbrush, hairbrush and comb, the matron led Joe to a wing of the home where the boys' bedrooms were located. Each room had as many single cots as the room would hold. They were arranged along the two, long, white walls. The room was very clean and orderly. At the foot of the bed was a trunk to hold their possessions and above each bed hung a plaque with a Bible verse on it. The verse above Joe's bed read;

> *Come unto me, all ye that labour and are heavy laden, and I will give you rest. Matthew 11:28 KJV*

"How many boys and girls are here?" Joe asked, finally finding his tongue. "There are a lot of beds."

The matron told him that this wing of the home had beds for close to one hundred boys. There were other wings at the opposite end of the home where there were bedrooms for the girls.

"What do they all do?" Joe asked.

"Were you told, here at Middlemore, you will be taught a trade?"

"No."

"Well, the boys all learn a skill, something they can eventually work at and earn money."

"And the girls?"

"The girls learn how to keep a proper home; to cook and clean a house. Girls are taught domestic work, and boys are taught a manual trade."

"Do they work all the time?"

The matron had just finished making up his little cot, covered with a grey blanket, the same as all the other little cots in the room. She looked up at this shy, skinny, little boy with all the questions and smiled. "There will be time to play. Sunday is a day of rest. But now you have an appointment to see the nurse back in the office. After that, I think it will be time for supper."

"Nurse?" Joe uttered quietly.

She either didn't hear or ignored him.

The nurse was gentle. She simply asked Joe more questions about whether he had ever had measles and mumps and other childhood diseases. She looked in his ears and throat, checked for infectious diseases and then wrote down his measurements after she had weighed him and measured his height. "How old did you say you were?" she asked, and shook her head when Joe answered, "nine."

Supper, at 5 o'clock was the biggest meal Joe had ever seen. There was a large plate of vegetables and rice and some meat, more

All Alone Again
Joe Payne, British Home Child

than he could possibly eat. He was seated at a long table, in the living room, with many other children. They were rather quiet for so many of them. Heads were bowed as they all said grace together.

> *"Be present at our table Lord*
> *Be here and everywhere adored*
> *These mercies bless, and grant that we*
> *May feast in paradise with thee."* *

"What's your name?" the boy beside him asked.

Before Joe could answer, the porter, who was responsible for keeping order, overheard and declared. "Children are to be seen and not heard."

It was later, after dark, when the children had said their prayers and were all in bed, that Joe felt terribly alone, even though he was in a room with twenty other boys in similar circumstances. He didn't recognize any of them, but he had learned a few names when they had played games after supper. He dug his fists into his eyes to hold back the tears. He didn't know that there were other boys in the room holding back their tears, trying as well, to be strong. Some were crying silently. If he heard a sniffle from time to time, he thought some boy had a cold.

The night was long, and Joe felt as if he had just got to sleep when it was time to get up again. At 6:30 AM it was still dark outside. The boys quickly got washed and dressed, made their beds and placed their neatly folded pajamas on the foot of their narrow little cots. Prayers were said, and they were in the living room, seated for breakfast by 7:30.

That morning Joe saw the boy who had sat beside him at supper the previous night. He told him, "I'm Joe Payne."

The boy, whose bed was three down, on the opposite side of the room, answered that his name was "Harold."

Harold was ten years old. He told Joe that he had a brother, James, who was eight, who slept in another bedroom. The brothers had been at the Middlemore home for about a month.

Harold told Joe that his brother had clung to him with his

- *Grace said at Middlemore Homes*

29

thumb in his mouth when they had first arrived. The matron had told Harold that at some point James would be going somewhere without his brother. It would be best for them to be separated right from the beginning so that one brother would not depend on the other. Another older boy was designated to watch out for James.

Breakfast, a good size bowl of porridge, was eaten quietly.

Joe was told he would attend the Hope Street School. Joe liked school. He was a smart boy and an excellent reader. He also liked working with numbers in arithmetic. He was quite often given a penny for having the best marks.

The children at Middlemore were encouraged with rewards. They were given a penny to spend on treats. Sometimes, when they didn't behave, they would not be allowed play time, but they were never spanked.

At noon, the children returned to the home for lunch and then went back to school for afternoon classes.

After school, Joe was told to spend some time doing chores. He was to help a chap called Robert. The home had a vegetable garden and some animals. Joe helped carry pails of feed for the animals and helped to clean out the stalls. He especially liked the rabbits, and would hold one big black fellow in his arms and stroke the long, silky, black ears.

Everything was all so new to Joe at Middlemore.

That autumn, Joe learned how to pick vegetables and store them for use in winter. In the spring, he learned how to plant the tiny seeds. Over the next eight months, he learned a lot about caring for animals.

On Sundays, they went to church and Sunday school. Other than when they were looking after the animals, they had free time to play. Some of the bigger boys were bullies, but Joe held his own. He counted the days until his mum would be well, and he could go home. The meals were good at the home, except for the rice. They had it every day. Joe swore once he left the home he would never eat rice again, and he never did.

Often Mr. Middlemore was at the home, and he would read them a story before bed. The story was often about orphaned children, like Joe, who were alone and bitter in the beginning but found a wonderful, loving home in the end.

All Alone Again
Joe Payne, British Home Child

In spring, they started to build a new hen house at Middlemore, and Joe was interested in the measurements. Robert showed him how to measure the boards they were to cut. Joe wasn't allowed to use the saw, but he was given a hammer when it was time to drive in the nails.

Joe thought that when he grew up he might like to build his own house. He would buy a little piece of land, and he would build a house for his mother and sister and himself to live in. He would have a garden in the back yard and grow lots of potatoes and carrots. He would have a cow to give them milk and some chickens to provide them with eggs.

Joe had resigned himself to Middlemore, learning what he could, behaving himself and staying out of the way of the bullies. He had come to trust the Middlemore staff. He was just biding his time, until his mum came to take him home.

"Today's the day," he thought when one day he was called to the office. However, he was not the only one beckoned. Half a dozen of the other boys entered with him. There was a doctor in the room who examined each one of them and filled out a paper with their name on it. Joe couldn't read what it said. The doctor closed the folder when he had seen all the boys. They were dismissed and another group of six boys was called to the office.

31

A few days later, over one hundred boys and girls were summoned and asked to go upstairs, pack all their belongings in a bag, put their Sunday clothes on, bring their coats and hats, and be back downstairs as quickly as possible.

A couple of the lads asked why, where were they going, but they got no reply. One hundred and twenty boys and girls, in total, all dressed in their best clothes with overcoats, hats and ties on, left Middlemore Home that afternoon in May 1915. They each carried a satchel, a type of suitcase with a shoulder strap, that held their few belongings; an extra suit which consisted of a brown cloth jacket and short pants, a vest, two extra shirts, three more pairs of long socks, two more collars, another cap, boots, two more handkerchiefs, a scarf and mittens, garters, a brush and comb and a toothbrush. One special item had been given to each child that lived at Middlemore Emigration Homes - a Bible. It was hoped that the child might find some small comfort in the Word of God. Inside the front cover a verse was written:

> *Be strong and of a good courage; be not afraid, neither be thou dismayed: for the Lord thy God is with thee whithersoever thou goest. Josiah 1:9 KJV*

The children walked to the train station, along with George Jackson and some other chaperones, believing they were headed on some exciting excursion.

It was an excursion all right. The train took them to Liverpool where they would be put aboard a ship going to Canada the following day. Arguing with the caretakers, that they didn't want to go, did no good. Joe couldn't make anyone listen when he told them his mum wouldn't know where he went.

Joe pieced together a few facts: the home had been training him to work on a farm in Canada, he was now ready, and his bed was needed for another boy coming to the home to learn how to farm.

"But, my mum," he tried to ask.

"Your mum has signed a paper for you to go to Canada," he was told. "It is a safer place for you to be. She wants you to go there."

"She doesn't want me." Joe thought. "How come she kept Ena and gave me away? I never wanted these clothes and food that Mr.

All Alone Again
Joe Payne, British Home Child

Middlemore gave me. Things were fine the way they were." He felt abandoned, forsaken and rejected. He didn't realize how ill his mother was. The decision had been taken out of her hands.

The children were given some final shots to prevent disease. Inspections were done by The Canadian Immigration officials. When they were deemed to be of good British stock, they were fed supper. They spent the night at Canada House with other children from other homes in England, similar to Middlemore.

The next morning the children were taken to the port to board a ship for Canada. It was May 18, 1915. They said goodbye to most of their chaperones from Middlemore. Only George Jackson would go to Canada with them. They had new escorts to cross the Atlantic Ocean with, two stewardesses, one for the girls and one for the boys.

SS Carthaginian
from Mariners Museum of Newport News, VA

Joe had never seen a ship before. The SS Carthaginian was so much bigger than he could ever imagine. It took two weeks to cross the Atlantic Ocean, but Joe was always sure it took a month. There were one hundred and fifty children on the ship headed for Canada. Canada had paid $2 a head for each child to come as a farm labourer or a domestic servant. The children were under contract to work, in return for their room and board, until they were eighteen years of age.

Carolyn MacIsaac

Joe was too seasick to enjoy the crossing. Some of the boys with better sea legs actually enjoyed touring the ship. They liked to watch the ocean for whales and porpoises. Sometimes they would pass another ship. The children slept below deck in bunks. There was a washroom with wash basins, soap, water, towels and a night commode. There were no windows.

Joe was on deck when they spotted land. The sun was shining on the water which made it glisten like silver. The heat from the sun felt good on his face and bare arms. They sailed into Halifax harbor, the deepest harbor in the world, on the first day of June in 1915 and glided into Pier 2.

PIER 2
HALIFAX, NS
Ships transporting British Home Children from Liverpool England arriving at Pier 2 in Halifax

Chapter 5

Canada
(June 1915)

Mr. and Mrs. Ray, caretakers from Fairview Home in Bedford, run by Middlemore Emigration Homes, met the children at the immigration shed at Pier 2. Nearly three million immigrants had entered Canada through this shed over the past twenty years. Mr. Ray was the superintendent, his wife the matron, and his sister, Mary Ann Pringle, the secretary at Fairview Home.

Mr. Ray took the hand of a little girl, and then as Joe staggered a little, Mr. Ray reached for his hand as well. Joe didn't have his land legs yet after being on a rocking ship for two weeks.

"There, there now lad. Take my hand, and we'll just stand off to one side while we wait for everyone to line up and be counted."

Mr. Ray looked down at Joe. "How was it, being on a big ship like the Carthaginian?" Did the captain allow you to be the helmsman and steer the ship?"

"No, sir. Freddy said he got to see this big wheel they steer the ship with, but me, I never did."

"And what did you do? Were there games to play?"

"There were games, but me, I liked to look out on the water. I saw three ships we met, and I think I saw maybe whales jumping in the water."

"They may have been whales, or they were more apt to have been porpoises. Porpoises often follow the ships. What about you missy?" Mr. Ray turned to the little girl whose hand he was holding on his other side. "What did you see on board the big ship?"

The little girl with her thumb in her mouth merely looked up with large round eyes and said nothing.

It was an hour later that the hungry, tired children with their caretakers reached Fairview Home.

Fairview was a receiving house for children, built on 50 acres of land, just outside the city of Halifax. It would accommodate 150 children. The children were to live in Fairview until they went to their new home. Some children would be there for only a day or two, while others might be there for months.

It was Mr. Middlemore who was responsible for selecting families for the children. He took the greatest care in sending the children to Christian families who would treat them as part of the family. They would be sent to school and taken to church. Mr. Ray, as superintendent, was responsible for visiting the children and sending monthly reports to England.

Mr. Ray was also responsible for sending monthly financial reports to England. Although there was a war, it had little effect on the home at that time as they presumed it would be over quickly. They raised their own chickens which gave them plenty of eggs, had a large vegetable garden, and had large bags of wheat, oatmeal and rice in storage. The children were fed nutritious food, and although they did chores, the Rays treated them kindly. Mr. Ray had been a British Home Child himself.

After being in the home for only a few days, Joe said goodbye to the boys he had grown closest to over the past year: Harold, John,

All Alone Again
Joe Payne, British Home Child

William and Arthur. Joe would never see any of them again. Of the hundred children who had crossed the Atlantic with Joe, some went to New Brunswick, some went to Prince Edward Island and some went to other parts of Nova Scotia. Bernard Duggan, Freddy Haywood, John William Ellis and another twenty boys and girls would be traveling part of the way with Joe to Cape Breton. Freddy had to say goodbye to his two brothers, Joseph and Ronald. They would be going in another direction.

Joe, with the other boys and girls and two caretakers, went by train from Halifax to Cape Breton. There, they would meet the farmers they would be working for until they were eighteen years of age.

The countryside they passed, for several hours, was nothing like crowded England. Joe, sitting by the window, saw nothing but trees most of the time. Even when the train stopped along the way, there was usually only a small station with few houses or stores to be seen.

Just before they reached Truro, Joe saw more houses than he had seen in the countryside they had just passed through. The Truro station itself was much larger than the others they had stopped at along the way, and there were more people coming and going. The train spent some time in Truro, but Joe, with his group, didn't get off. Some of the cars were separated to head towards Quebec and Ontario. The car Joe was on headed towards Cape Breton.

When the train left Truro, it once again passed miles and miles of just trees, stopping a few more times to let people off or pick them up before they reached the next town of Stellarton. It was a larger station, much like Truro, and there were more houses to be seen. Not far past Stellarton was New Glasgow, and an hour later the town of Antigonish, larger stations with more people coming and going. But these Maritime stations were nothing in size compared to the one back home in Birmingham, England.

At mealtime, the caretakers took the children to the dining car for something to eat. Joe swayed from side to side as they moved along. The food served was much like something you would get in any restaurant. The anxious little boys and girls barely ate a bite. They were scared and nervous and had butterflies in their tummies.

Carolyn MacIsaac

When the train reached the Northumberland Strait, a body of water which separated Cape Breton from the mainland of Nova Scotia, the train was carried by ferry to Cape Breton Island. In another thirty-five years the ferry would be replaced by a causeway. The station here was unique in that trains in both directions reversed into the station because they could not be turned on the Cape Breton side of the Strait.

The train carrying ferry went from the Mulgrave Station on the mainland of Nova Scotia to the Point Tupper Station on the island. Once on the other side, the train would continue on the mainline towards Sydney.

The caregivers, along with the boys and girls, got off in Port Hawkesbury. Joe was told to sit on a bench with some of the other children. The children were silent as they waited while Bernie, John and Freddy were handed off to the farmers they would be working for. If any of them said goodbye, it was said so quietly that no one heard. Bernie went to live in River Denys, John William with a family in Jubilee, and Freddy with a McInnis family in Orangedale. Even though all three boys were settled in Inverness County, Joe would never see any of them again. For the past year, they had had each other. It had helped the home sickness to know that others were in the same boat. As each child was passed off to the farmer they would be serving, the loneliness dug deeper in Joe's soul.

Before long, Joe, with just a few of the other children and one caretaker, was headed towards Inverness on the opposite side of the island. The Inverness & Richmond railway ran sixty miles along the

All Alone Again
Joe Payne, British Home Child

coast of the Northumberland Strait from Port Hawkesbury to Inverness. The line had opened on June 15, 1901, to serve coal mines in Inverness and Mabou which were owned by the Canadian National Light Locomotives Railway. Despite its name, the line would never extend into Richmond County.

Neil MacInnis was standing on the platform in Mabou when the train arrived. It was just a coincidence that he had the same last name as the family Freddy had been left with. They were not related. Neil looked eagerly as each person exited the train. He was beginning to think the boy he had requested hadn't arrived. He hoped nothing terrible had happened. A few weeks back, on May 7th, a British passenger ship had been torpedoed by a German submarine and twelve hundred passengers had been lost at sea. Neil was thinking about this when a middle-aged gentleman asked if he was Neil MacInnis.

Neil looked from the man to the small boy questioningly as he answered, "yes".

"Here is your ward, Joseph." The man said. "Joseph, this is your guardian, Neil MacInnis."

"There must be a mistake." Neil answered, ignoring Joe. "I am to meet a seventeen- year-old boy to help with farm work."

"I am sorry," the man said. "This time, the boys that were sent, were all young. Joe is a good healthy boy and a lot stronger than he looks. He will serve you well. He just needs a few good meals to fatten him up."

Neil argued to no avail that he couldn't possibly take this small child home to his mother. She would have a fit. The boy could be of no use, and the last thing they needed was another mouth to feed. The man reminded Neil that a contract had been signed, so it was left that Joe would go on to the farm with Mr. MacInnis for the time being. Later on, he could be sent back to Fairview in Halifax and exchanged for another boy.

The caretaker had to get back on the train quickly to accompany the other children, who would be taken all the way to Inverness. Then he would head back to Halifax and prepare for the next shipment of British Home Children sent to Canada. Between 1869 and 1939 over 100,000 children would be sent overseas. Many came from Middlemore Emigration Homes. Others came from other emigration homes such as Barnardo.

Joe was never to see any of the other children again! None that he recognized at least.

With his little suitcase in hand, Joe got in a buggy standing nearby.

"What am I to do with you now?" Neil asked as they drove along.

Joe looked down at his feet. He was determined not to cry. He had heard what had been said between this man and the caregiver from Middlemore. He couldn't open his mouth to answer.

It was dark by the time they reached the little farmhouse. The horses knew where to turn off the road to the right and go up the long driveway to the barn.

Inside the house, the girls were asleep upstairs. Christy was sitting in a rocking chair, by the stove in the kitchen when Neil entered with the exhausted little boy. Here things went from bad to worse for Joe, as the conversation between Neil and his mother was spoken in Gaelic, the Scottish language that most of Cape Breton spoke.

Although Joe couldn't make out a word, he could gather that Mrs. MacInnis was even less pleased than her son had been, with this young waif from England.

Not sure if he was coming or going, Joe was eventually shown to a small room upstairs where he would at least spend the night. It was late, and he got ready for bed quickly. There was certainly no hugging or tucking in. The room was pitch black once the candle was removed. Was this what hell was like? He couldn't even see his hand if he held it up in front of him. No one came to comfort him as he lay there in the dark crying his heart out!

Chapter 6

Glenville, Cape Breton (1915 -1920)

Joe awoke to the sound of creaking stairs. He was thinking he had to get up and go to the outside toilet when the door was flung open, and Neil entered his tiny room.

"Time to get up and at it," Neil said. "Might as well find out what good stock you come from. Have you ever seen a farm before?"

Joe answered that he had learned to farm at Middlemore. He was determined to be as useful as he could. What would happen to him if he was sent back to Fairview? He didn't know.

Joe got dressed, went to the outside toilet and then followed Neil to a nearby field. A large beige dog joined them. The dog sniffed

Carolyn MacIsaac

at Joe. Neil gave the dog a pat. "This is Buddy," he said. "He rounds up the sheep and the cows."

It was still dark, but Joe could see the sun would be rising shortly. There was a light mist in the air, but Joe faintly made out a large barn to his left and a brook nearby running across the back of the property. On the other side of the brook loomed a mountain. The MacInnis farm was in a large open space in a valley. Looking all around, Joe could see only one other house. This was so different from the life he had known back in England where houses were practically piled on top of each other. In Birmingham, there had been so many people crowded together, it was rare to be able to see even a blade of grass. Here, in Canada, there seemed to be tall, green grass, wet from the dew, everywhere.

Neil opened the gate and led a couple dozen cows back to the barn. Mary joined them, and she and Neil milked the cows. Neil had Joe fill buckets of grain. Joe was then shown how to feed the cows in order to keep them calm as they were being milked.

Mary kept an eye on Joe but didn't speak to him. She and her brother were busy getting the morning chores done as quickly as possible. When they did speak, they conversed in Gaelic.

Joe tried to be as helpful as possible and did as he was told to the best of his ability. He proved to be an excellent worker for a boy only nine, and even more so because he looked so frail.

Joe's stomach growled. He had eaten so little the day before.

Back at the farmhouse, Joe watched as Neil and Mary pumped water from the well to wash, then he did the same.

Inside, Mrs. MacInnis, or Ma as she was called by the children, was busy at the stove. A girl about Joe's age was finishing setting the table. Ma gestured for Joe to sit at the table; four other girls joined them. One of the girls was younger than Joe but much bigger. The meal was ingested quietly after Neil said something in Gaelic. Joe presumed it was grace, giving thanks to the Lord, for the food.

There was cream and brown sugar to put on the porridge. Joe enjoyed every bite. He watched while Neil took a piece of bread and spread butter and molasses on it. After one of the girls did the same she passed the plate of bread to Joe. They all drank a cup of tea. Joe's and the younger girls' had lots of milk in it. Even though the

All Alone Again
Joe Payne, British Home Child

MacInnis family was poor, there was always milk and butter and even cream to pour on porridge.

Joe turned to Neil and asked him what work he had for him that morning.

Neil kept a straight face as he answered in English. "I am going to get you to lift the house up in the air while I replace a beam under it."

Joe was afraid he was serious, but the girls giggled.

Gaelic was always spoken at home, and English was taught at school so the children were bilingual.

Joe soon picked up a few Gaelic words himself. Thank you was "tapadh leat," and please was "ma'se do thoile."

Joe followed Neil around the remainder of his first day on the farm. The four younger children spent the morning in school, came home for lunch, and went back to school for the afternoon. Mary helped her mother inside the house in the morning, and in the afternoon she worked alongside her brother planting beans. Mary showed Joe how to drop a tiny bean in the middle of the long rows they had made. She would walk behind Joe, cover the bean with soil and ever so gently pat it down.

"You must never look back when you are planting, Joe," she said. "If you do, the row will be crooked."

Mary told Joe that they had already planted some crops. "The beans don't go in the ground until after the full moon in June. Often we get frost at the time of the full moon, and it will kill the tiny plants. We will plant beans again in a couple of weeks. That way we will eat fresh string beans, some yellow and some green until September. Then we will pick the remainder and dry them in the sun. The seeds will be stored to make baked beans throughout the winter. Some dried beans will be saved for planting next summer."

All the hard work was making Joe hungry again.

Mary continued, "We planted rows and rows of potatoes last week. We grow enough and store them in the cold cellar to last all winter. Potatoes have to be planted when there is a new moon in the sky. Potatoes grow with the moon."

Joe wasn't sure if Mary was pulling his leg or not, but through time he heard it said often enough that he believed it himself, and always planted his potatoes when there was a new moon.

As they were planting row after long row of string beans, Mary asked Joe if he had ever eaten blue potatoes.

"No" he answered, "never did."

"Ma always cooks blue potatoes when we have fish."

Joe learned to love blue potatoes. Ma would soak dried codfish overnight before she cooked it. She would make a white sauce with flour and butter and milk to mix with the fish. This was poured over the blue potatoes. It became a favorite meal for Joe. Sometimes they had herring. Joe liked that too, except for all the bones.

The family went to Inverness every Saturday afternoon for groceries. Although they grew their own vegetables and cured their own meat, they needed to buy some things such as flour and molasses in bulk. Christy would take a metal container from home and the storekeeper would pour the rich golden liquid from the large molasses barrel into it. Flour and sugar came in large cloth bags that could be used as pillowcases when they were empty.

Sunday morning, the whole family was up early, as usual, to get the farm chores done. After breakfast, they got cleaned up and put their best clothes on. Joe wore the clothes he had worn on Sundays at Middlemore. Neil hitched the horses to the buggy, and they rode to the little Presbyterian Church in Strathlorn.

Partway through the service, officiated by Reverend Donald J. Morrison, Joe went downstairs with the younger children for Sunday school. Over the next few years, he would attend church regularly. Although it was a stipulation of Middlemore that the children be taken to church, the MacInnis family had always attended faithfully. Neil was even Sunday School Superintendent. Joe received several diplomas for memorizing Bible verses with Neil's signature on them. October 2, 1921, he would receive one for memorizing the whole of the shorter catechism plus an additional 150 verses.

The family always spoke Gaelic when Ma was around, but Joe learned a little about the way of life on the farm when he worked side by side with the girls. He didn't attend school in June, and classes were soon finished until September.

All Alone Again
Joe Payne, British Home Child

Carolyn MacIsaac

All Alone Again
Joe Payne, British Home Child

There was always lots of work for everyone throughout the summer. There wasn't much time for play. Other than necessary barn chores, making of meals and cleaning up, Sunday was the Lord's Day, and no other work or play was encouraged. There might be a day or two in July or August when the children would wade in the brook to get cooled off. There might be a few times in the winter when the children would coast down a hill. There were a few times, but not often, that Joe got to play ball with Malcolm. Malcolm lived on the farm next door. He had no friends other than the girls in the family.

Joe wasn't long at the farm before William Ray, from the Middlemore Home in Halifax, came to visit. Mr. Ray was concerned that they might not be keeping the little boy he had left with them. Joe seemed in good health and still had clothing he had brought from England that fit. He was attending church and would attend school later. At his age, it was expected that in lieu of wages he would only receive room and board. Overall, Mr. Ray wrote on the report that the home was fairly satisfactory and the MacInnis family were keeping Joe.

When the crops were all put in, Joe helped Neil with fencing. The snow that came every winter would knock some of the fences to the ground. Neil had repaired those that were in the worst shape, but there were always more to be replaced. Neil had cut down trees in winter for firewood and put aside some of the smaller ones to make fence posts. These he cut in six and a half foot lengths and peeled the bark off. One end of the new post was sharpened with an axe to make it easier to stick in the ground. If the old post was broken it was usually easier to dig a new hole for the new post. Joe would dig a hole a couple feet, and then Neil would use a digging bar to go deeper at the center. Neil would then hold the new post in place while Joe packed the mud back in around it. Barbed wire was run between the posts to deter the animals from climbing over and leaving the property. There were separate pastures for the horses, cattle, sheep and one bull.

Joe had been at the farm two months when there was a heat wave. The upstairs bedrooms were stifling. There was no insulation in the walls of the house, so it was hot in summer in contrast to winter when there would be frost on the inside walls. It was difficult to sleep at night. It would be midnight before the temperature lowered and a small breeze would come in through open windows. Everyone was lethargic from heat and lack of sleep.

Christy used the stove as little as possible. She would start a wood fire as early as possible in the morning, and get as little baking as she could get away with, done quickly.

The sweat was running down Alena's neck as she finished the midday dishes. "Do you think Ma will let us take a dip in the brook?" she said to Jessie.

"She might," Jessie said, "if you ask her."

"Ma," Alena said, "if we promise not to get our clothes muddy can we please go in the brook to get cooled off?" Alena was standing in the doorway between the pantry and the kitchen.

"Oh Alena, I know you are hot, but you will get your clothes wet, and it will make more work to wash them and iron them again."

Christine heard the conversation between her mother and her younger sister and butted in.

"Ma, I will wash the dresses, and hang them out to dry right after we get back to the house. I will iron them early in the morning while the stove is hot. I promise." In the days before electricity, the iron was heated by setting it on the hot stove.

"You'll have to get up extra early."

"Yes Ma, please? Christine said. "It will be worth it just to get cooled off today. I won't mind getting up at five. We don't sleep very well upstairs in this heat anyway."

"Please, Ma?" Alena begged.

The other children were huddled behind the door listening.

Christy turned to her son who was sitting at the table looking through a catalog.

"You'll be needing the girls to help with the haying this afternoon, I imagine?"

"Actually," he responded, "I need to go into town this afternoon and find new teeth for the mower before I do any more cutting, and the hay we cut yesterday won't be ready to put in the barn until at least tomorrow."

The MacInnis family had started haying when the grass had begun to flower around the middle of July. Neil would cut the tall grass with the sickle bar mower hauled by two workhorses. The freshly cut hay would lay on the ground for a couple of days to dry or

All Alone Again
Joe Payne, British Home Child

cure as they called it before the children would rake it in piles, throw it on the wagon using a three-pronged pitchfork, and then take it to the barn where it would be stored in the hayloft. If the hay wasn't dried before it was stored, it could go moldy but worse than that it would cause the temperature in the barn to rise to a dangerous level and start a fire. Normally Neil would be cutting hay in one field using two of the workhorses while the girls would be with the other two horses in another field lugging dry hay to the barn. The horses worked hard all day hauling the hay to the barn. A pitchfork was used to take the hay off the wagon and store it in the hayloft in the barn.

"All right then," Christy sighed, "as long as Neil doesn't need your help you may go in the brook for an hour. But no mess now."

"Can Joe come too? Alena asked.

"Joe has to help Neil this afternoon."

"I don't need Joe to come along," Neil answered. "He's not much good to me in this heat. He tells me it doesn't get this sunny and hot in England. It might cheer him up to get wet in the brook."

Christy sighed. "Ah well then, it looks like you all have your heart set on it, so go ahead, but remember no mess and be back here at three." She was so hot herself, she just wanted to sit and fan herself.

So Joe got to go in the brook with the girls. There was one spot where the water was a couple feet deep right in the middle. They walked in cautiously, sharp stones digging in their feet. They didn't have bathing suits so they were wearing their everyday clothes. The water felt cold at first, and soon lowered their body temperature. They splashed around and sprayed each other for a good part of an hour. When they came out of the water, they walked slowly back to the house, the sun drying their clothes as they went. They were careful not to get the wet clothes dirty, and they were dry by the time they returned home.

Just as his Mum had daydreamed, Joe did get to pick apples off the trees in the orchard beside the house. Sometimes, Buddy, the dog would be by his side. His favorite apple came from the August apple tree. They were yellow and ripened earlier than the others. It was important to pick the apples before they fell to the ground. Once the apples were on the ground, worms would quickly find their way into them and leave little tracks all over the apple. Ma, with the girl's help, would make enough apple jelly to last all winter. It was good on

Carolyn MacIsaac

freshly baked bread, hot from the oven, maybe even better than the apple pie they sometimes had for dessert at Sunday dinner. A dish of applesauce was also a favorite with freshly baked biscuits.

Joe's favorite time of day was after the evening chores were done. The children would walk up the road, past the school, to get the mail. There was a post office in one of the farmhouses. Often Malcolm MacKinnon, the boy at the farm next door, would join them. The children would laugh and play along the way. It was daylight in summer, but come fall they were going for the mail after dark.

One night, when there was a harvest moon and the sky was full of stars, Hughena pointed out the big dipper and little dipper to Joe. She showed him where the North Star was at the end of the handle of the little dipper. "The North Star always points north," she said. "Its real name is Polaris, and all the stars in the Northern Hemisphere circle around it, while it remains stationary. It is very useful for navigation. I'll bet they watched for it on the ship you came to Canada on, Joe. It probably kept you on course so you didn't end up in South America." The children all stood and turned as she pointed to the north. "England is to the east," she said as she tentatively looked at Joe. The others all looked at Joe, feeling sorry for him. How he must miss his home they thought.

Joe did look sad, and he looked longingly towards the east as Hughena pointed in that direction.

"Did you see the moon in England, Joe?'

He nodded his head.

"It is the same moon. There is only one. Just think, maybe your mum is looking up at the same moon in the sky right now. Does that make you feel closer to her?"

Joe didn't answer. He didn't know if it made him feel closer or further away. He felt like he was a different person now in a different life. After looking at the moon for another moment he turned and said, "Race you to the next driveway," and he raced on ahead of the others.

Joe soon learned enough Gaelic that he could speak a little in the Scottish language. The common greeting for hello, how are you was "ciamar a tha thu?" and you're welcome was "ceud mile failte". Jessie told him that "thu" was used in a more casual way when he met other young people going for the mail. When speaking to Ma or other

All Alone Again
Joe Payne, British Home Child

adults at church, he should address them as "sibh". He learned to say my name is Joseph, "is mise Joseph" and I'm from England, "tha mi a England."

When if he was asked in Gaelic, if he would like a little more potatoes, he would answer "tha, beagan," yes, a little. When he went to bed at night he would say "Feasgar math," good night.

One night, when they were walking back from getting the mail, the girls taught him how to ask for something in Gaelic. Sometimes he had a question for Ma and didn't know how to ask it. She was a very strict woman, not just with him but with her own children as well. She probably had to be, a widow running a farm with the help of her son, five daughters and now a small boy from another country.

Joe on the far left with Alena and Hughena MacInnis and Silas MacKinnon (Silas was Mary Sarah's step-son)

When the haying and harvest were finished in the fall and put away for winter, Joe still couldn't go to school. He had to pick stones. It seemed every year more and more stones would work their way up to the top of the soil in the garden. Joe would pick them into a wheelbarrow, and when it got so heavy he could hardly push it, he

Carolyn MacIsaac

would wheel it to the side of the garden and make a fence with the stones.

Only on a rainy or snowy day was Joe allowed to go to school. School took in at nine o'clock and let out at three thirty. There were no scribblers or pencils. Each child, there were twenty-three of them, from grade primary to grade ten, had a slate. It was like a scribbler sized chalkboard that they wrote on with a piece of chalk. At lunchtime, they would walk home for something to eat. If it was a stormy day they might carry a biscuit with molasses on it and stay at school. If the weather cleared up by lunchtime, Joe would often have to stay at home in the afternoon to do farm work.

When the weather turned cold, some animals would be slaughtered for food. The dead animal would hang from a hook in the barn for a few days before it was cut up. There were three large wooden barrels in a small building just off the porch. One barrel was for lamb, one for pork and one for beef. Each container was filled with a salt brine after it was filled with the fresh meat. This would keep the meat from going bad in the days when there was no electricity. The wood for burning in the stove was stored in another part of the same building. It was near the house so they could get both meat and fuel easily.

Another way the MacInnis family had for storing meat was by using ice. In the winter, large slabs of ice would be cut from the lake. There was a large hole dug beside the woodshed and it was filled with layers of ice and sawdust. The ice would slowly melt in the summer, but it would usually last until the beginning of fall. In summer, a large block of ice would be placed in the ice chest to keep milk and cooked meat from spoiling. New ice would be added each week.

In winter, when there was snow on the ground they would hitch the horses to the sleigh instead of the wagon for travel to town or church.

Joe helped Neil cut wood all winter. It came from a forest on the opposite side of the road from their house. This was besides Joe looking after four horses, eighteen to twenty cows, and forty sheep; feeding them and cleaning out the barn. In winter he also had to dig a hole in the ice in the brook to get water for the animals. This was all done before he went to school, on a day that he was able to attend school.

All Alone Again
Joe Payne, British Home Child

In the middle of December, Joe experienced his first blizzard. "Looks like a blizzard out there today, Joe," Neil stated. Joe couldn't see a thing when he looked out the window. They waited in the kitchen for Mary and Christine, and then Neil told them to dress warmly and make sure they covered their faces with a scarf.

Neil pushed hard to open the back door against a good foot of snow that had already fallen throughout the night. He held the lantern high as they walked to the barn, Joe holding the scarf against his face with one hand and holding unto Neil's coat with his other hand. Christine had a hold of Neil's coat on the other side, and Mary held unto Christine.

The snow swirled around them, and although the barn was only a couple hundred feet away it seemed to take a long time to plunge through the snow to get there. Once inside, the four of them stood trying to catch their breath for a few minutes. The cows were milked and the animals fed quickly, and they returned to the house carrying the fresh milk with them. Daylight was beginning to creep in, and although it had a pinkish tinge they still couldn't see a foot in front of them.

Back in the farmhouse, Christy had a roaring fire going to warm the frozen fingers coming in from the storm. The hot tea and warm porridge had never tasted better.

There was no going to school for anyone that day. Alena was learning multiplication tables so she and Joe would test each other throughout the morning. The two times and five times tables and even the nine times tables were easy to remember, but they both struggled with six times seven, seven times nine and a few others. Joe was determined that Alena was not going to do better than him just because she got to go to school while he had to stay home and work. Over and over again, he said to himself all morning, six times seven is forty-two, so that by lunchtime when Alena said, "Joe, what is six times seven?" He answered quickly, with a smile on his face, "six times seven is forty-two. What is six times eight?"

The storm seemed to be over. Joe was mesmerized as he looked out the window. Everywhere you looked it was white, beautiful fresh, clean white snow. It wasn't just on the ground; the trees were heavy laden with snow on their branches as well. It was a winter wonderland.

Carolyn MacIsaac

Christy was busy separating the milk in the porch. She noticed Joe going back to look out the window from time to time. "I wonder if the lad's ever been coasting," she said.

"Oh yes, we should go coasting," the girls chimed in at once.

"This afternoon you are going to help me churn butter and get all this milking equipment washed up, then it will be time to make supper. Perhaps after supper, when the chores are done you may go."

So it was that Joe and the girls bundled up after dark and headed over to invite Malcolm along. The sky was bright with a full moon to light their way. It was hard trudging through two feet of snow. They often had to walk around some deep drifts. They drug behind them a double runner sled. It was one long sleigh made by joining two smaller sleds together using long boards. Their father had made it for them.

There was a hill across the road from the farm perfect for coasting. It was quite a walk to the top of the hill as they had to break a path in the snow. Christine got on the sled first, then Malcolm with his feet wrapped around Christine, then Alena and then Joe. Joe held on for dear life. There was room for everyone on the sleigh but they took turns so that the sleigh would glide over the hard crust and not sink. It was a cold evening, the children could see their breath. The sled zipped down the hill. The wind was on their faces, and it was exhilarating. Then they had to get off the sled and walk back up the hill. Joe didn't mind climbing back up the hill with fingers and toes that were frozen. There were moments that he was happy, that he forgot who he was, where he came from. Moments.

Joe was more fortunate than most of the British Home Children. He knew his mother's address back in England, and Neil helped him buy postcards to mail to her and his little sister, Ena, who was also called Maudie. Maud was the middle name of both Ena and her mother. Over time a scrapbook was bought for Joe to keep all the postcards he received from both his Mum and Ena. Mr. and Mrs. Ray also mailed Joe a Christmas card every year. He kept every one of them in the scrapbook.

All Alone Again
Joe Payne, British Home Child

THOUGH THE WIDE SEAS ROLL BETWEEN US (2)

Though the wide seas roll between us, I am thinking still of you,
I can hear your dear voice calling, and I know your heart is true;
When the parting days are over, through the sunshine and the rain
Though the wide seas roll between us now, they'll bear you home again.

BAMFORTH (copyright). By permission of J. H. Larway Wells St., Oxford St., London, W.1

Carolyn MacIsaac

Christmas cards from Mr. and Mrs. Ray, Fairview Home, Bedford, Nova Scotia, 1915 and 1917

All Alone Again
Joe Payne, British Home Child

Mrs. MacGregor may have worked at Fairview Home.

57

Carolyn MacIsaac

From Joe's mother

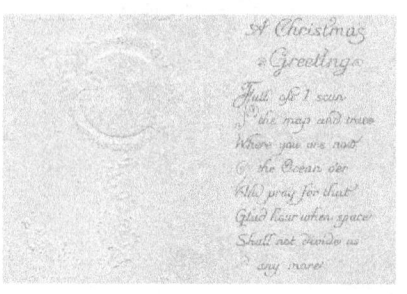

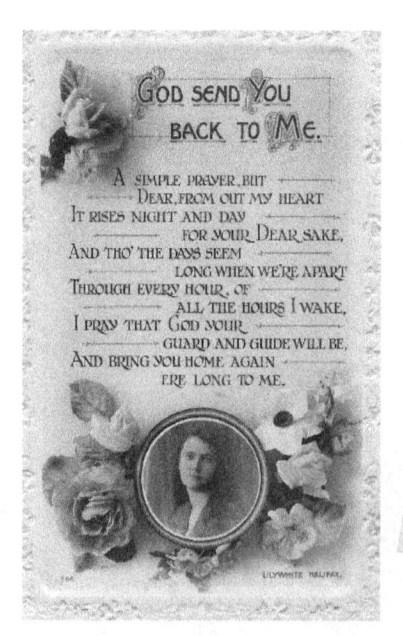

All Alone Again
Joe Payne, British Home Child

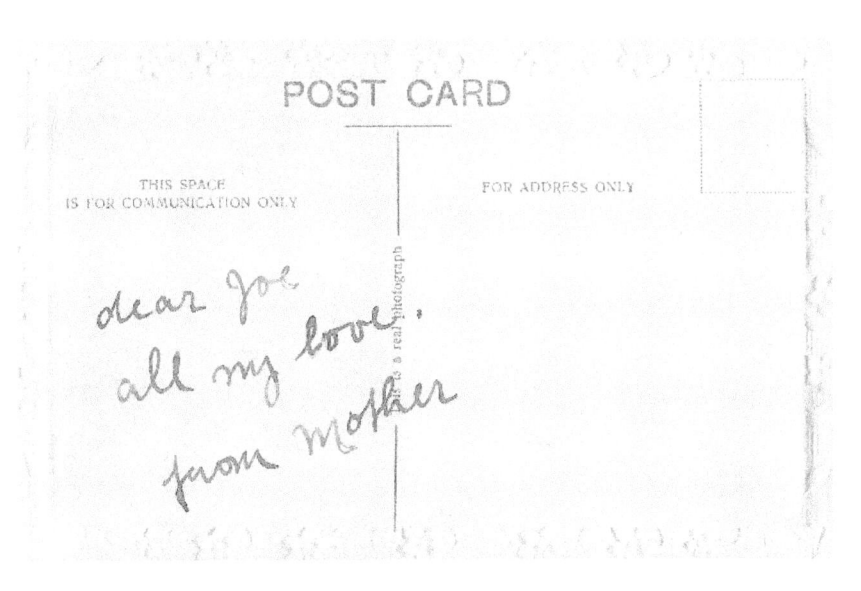

Loving Birthday Wishes To my dear Son

*A loving greeting and a wish sincere
This simple card conveys,
And may it bring you health and wealth
For many happy days.*

dear Joe,
all my love,
from Mother

Carolyn MacIsaac

All Alone Again
Joe Payne, British Home Child

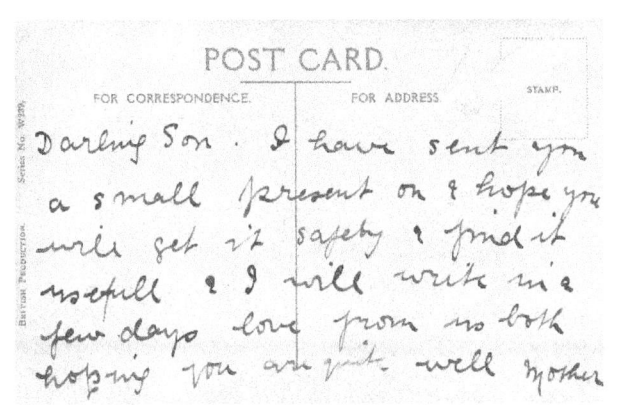

To My Son.

Dear Lad, I send this Bonnie Card, With its simple little rhyme, To tell you that your mother's heart is with you all the time.

POST CARD.

Darling Son. I have sent you a small present on & hope you will get it safety & find it usefull & I will write in a few days love from us both hoping you are quite well mother

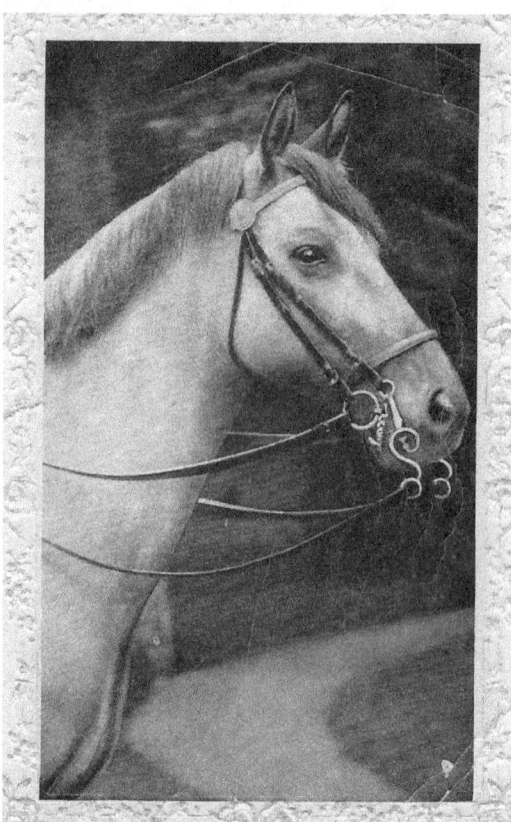

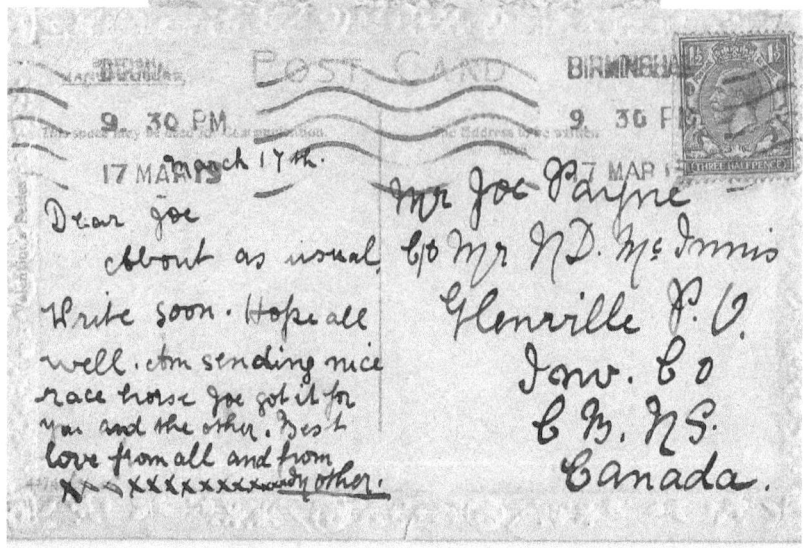

Carolyn MacIsaac

March 17th.

Dear Joe
About as usual. Write soon. Hope all well. Am sending nice race horse Joe got it for you and the other. Best love from all and from X oxxxxxxxxx and other.

Mr Joe Payne
c/o Mr N.D. McInnis
Glenville P.O.
Inv. Co
C.B. N.S.
Canada.

All Alone Again
Joe Payne, British Home Child

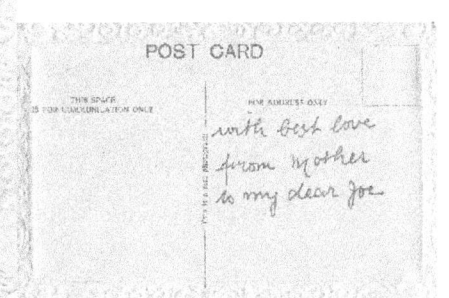

Carolyn MacIsaac

All Alone Again
Joe Payne, British Home Child

Carolyn MacIsaac

In ye olden Dayes.

Corporation Street.

Aston Hall.

Old Square.

All Alone Again
Joe Payne, British Home Child

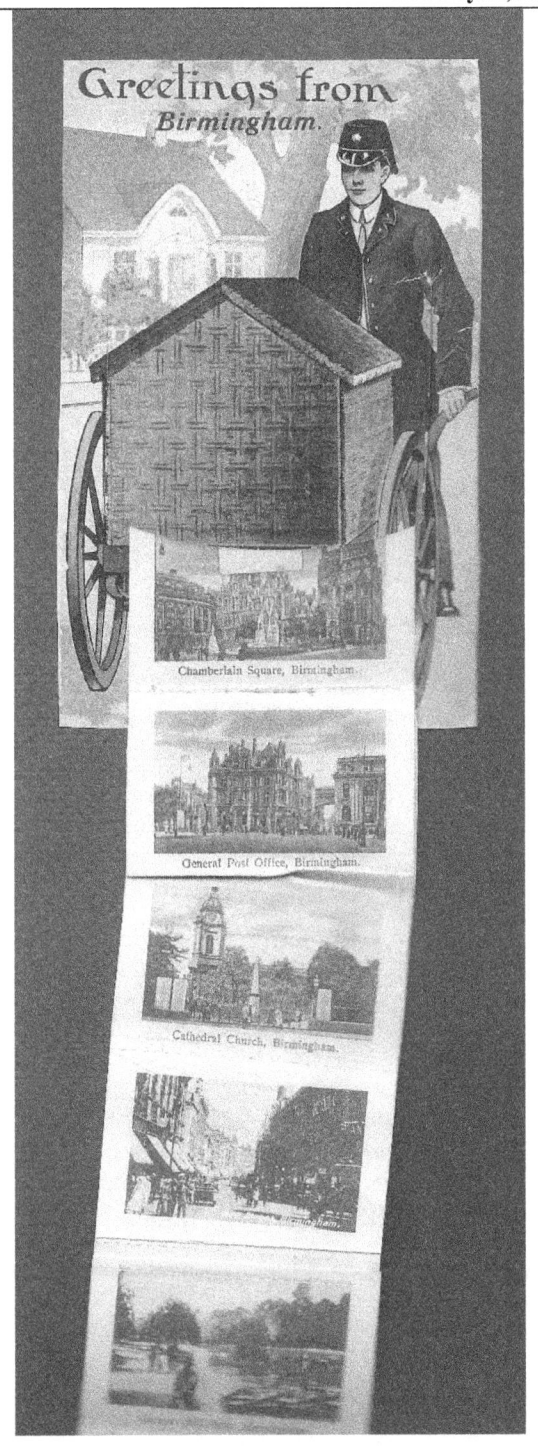

Carolyn MacIsaac

All Alone Again
Joe Payne, British Home Child

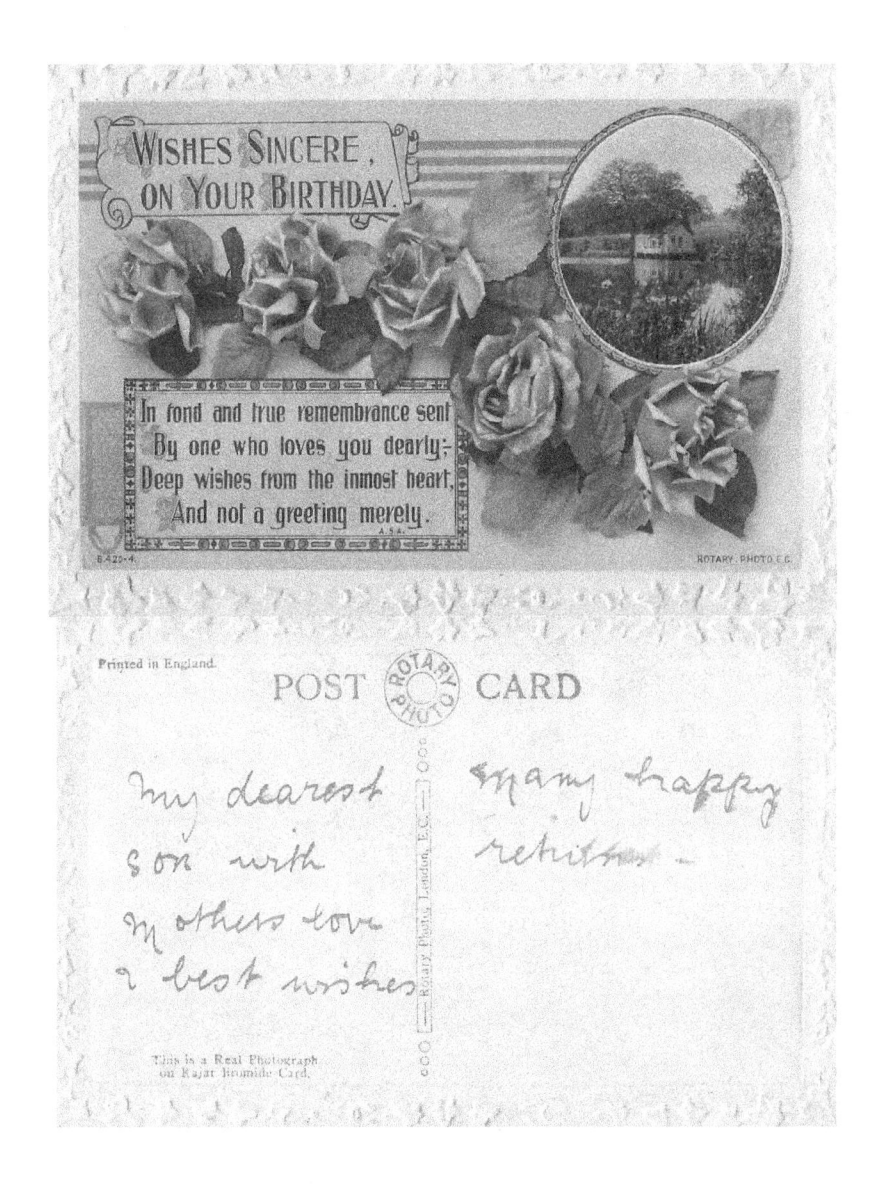

Carolyn MacIsaac

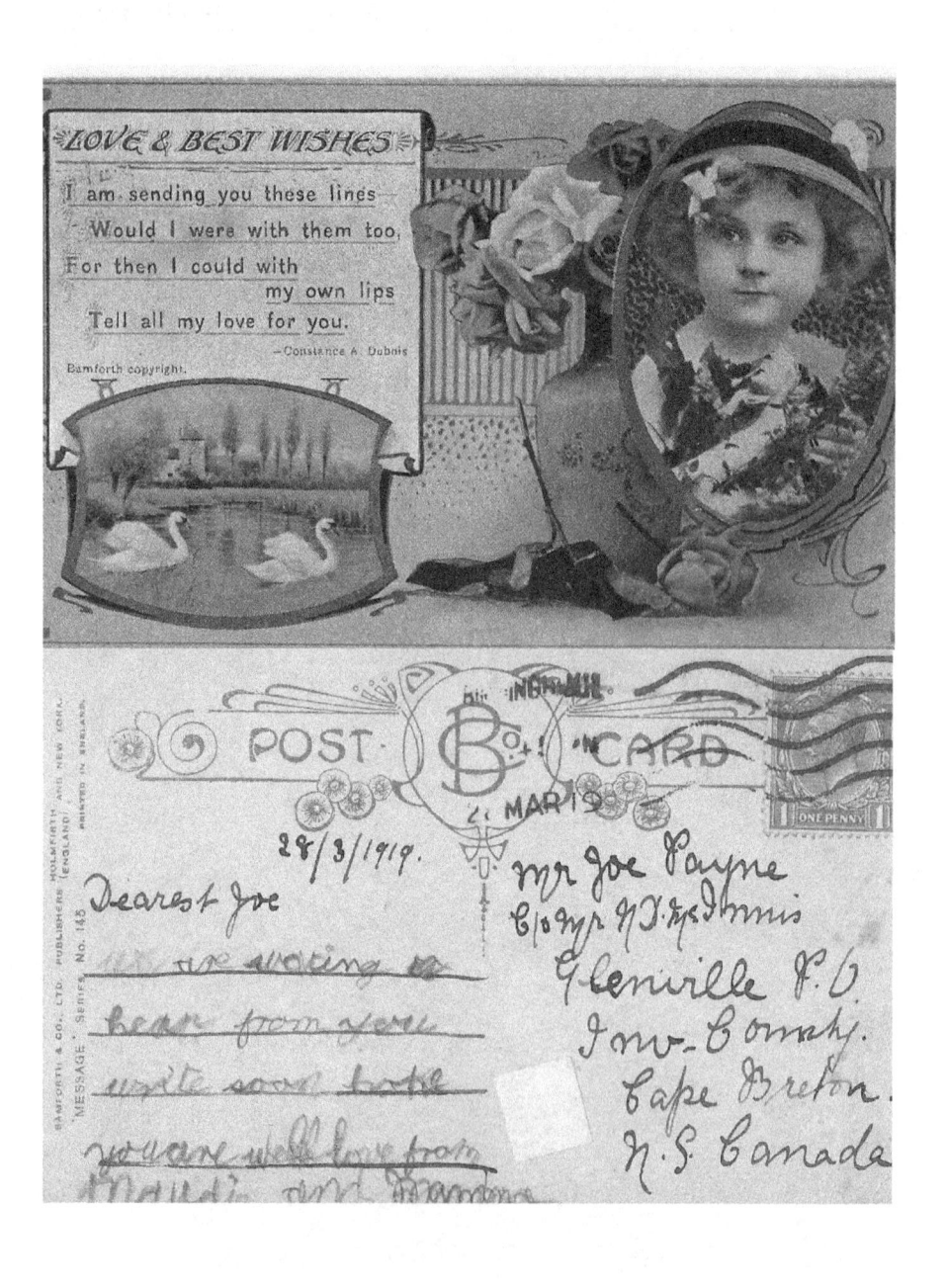

LOVE & BEST WISHES

I am sending you these lines
Would I were with them too,
For then I could with
           my own lips
Tell all my love for you.
— Constance A. Dubois

28/3/1919

Dearest Joe
we are waiting to
hear from you
write soon both
you are well love from
Maudie and mamma

Mr Joe Payne
C/o Mr N J McInnis
Glenville P.O.
Inv- County.
Cape Breton.
N.S. Canada

All Alone Again
Joe Payne, British Home Child

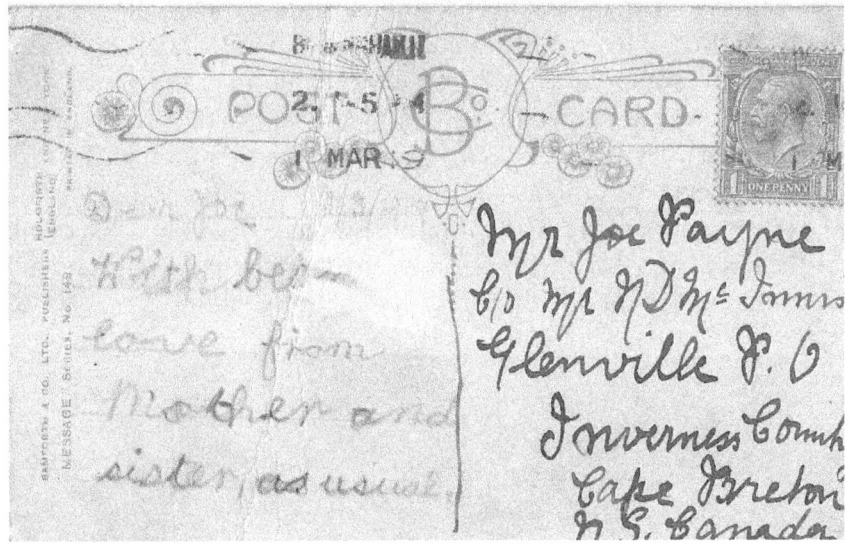

Mr. Ray, or one of his workers came to visit Joe every summer to see how he was doing on the farm. The British Home Children were never left alone with the visitors from Middlemore, so they never felt free to complain about their hard life. I am sure Mr. Ray knew that life was hard for them and how terribly homesick they were. However, Joe was being fed, had a bed to sleep in and was

71

attending church. In July of 1916, it was George Jackson who filled out the report. He didn't see Joe as he was three to five miles away picking berries. George found the home satisfactory. Mrs. MacInnis said the child was a nice little boy although he was a bit careless with his lessons. She said Joe was in good health and attended church and school. He was growing fast and they had to get him clothes as he had outgrown the ones he brought from England.

Joe had been on the farm two years when there was an explosion in Halifax. Two boats collided in the harbour on December 6, 1917. One boat was carrying explosives headed for the battlefields of the war. The explosion was felt all the way to Cape Breton. There had been a tsunami where all the water left the harbour and then came rushing back in. The north end of Halifax was completely wiped out. Nearly two thousand people died, and another nine thousand were maimed or blinded. More than twenty-five thousand people were left without adequate shelter.

Ma was persuaded to take in a little orphan boy named Clifford Collins. His parents had died in the Halifax explosion. Clifford had a brother taken in by another family in Cape Breton. Joe felt that Clifford was shown more love by the family than he had been shown on his arrival. One might wonder if there was a difference between a Canadian orphan and a street urchin from England who was under contract to work for them almost like a servant. Nevertheless it was fun having another boy to laugh and carry on with as the children went on their evening walks for the mail.

Joe, Christy, Hughena, Clifford, Alena and Neil

All Alone Again
Joe Payne, British Home Child

November 11, 1918, the war was finally over. Joe was now thirteen years old. He still had five more years to work on the farm serving the MacInnis family.

It wasn't until the end of November in 1918, when they had their yearly visit from Middlemore. Since no one was at home, Neil wrote them.

> *In answer to your inquiry, I wish to say that Joe is strong and healthy, attended school six months last term, always goes regularly, is very happy and contented, attends church and Sunday School, just now our church is vacant.*

September 5, 1919 Mr. Ray once again visited the MacInnis farm. He found everything appeared to be alright. Joe's health was good and he was attending church. He found his school attendance, his clothing, his home and surroundings very fair.

By the time Joe was big enough to handle the horse and buggy, Neil had a job working in the mine in Inverness. It became Joe's job to pick Neil up Saturday afternoon at the mine and bring him home for the night. He would take him back to the mine on Sunday afternoons. With Neil working away from home it meant more farm work for Joe. He was certainly earning his room and board.

Joe also sent postcards to his mother and sister in England.

Carolyn MacIsaac

wishing you a Merry Xmas and a Happy New Year Xmas 1924 From brother Joseph

Mistress Maud Payne

I hope you will have a Merry Xmas and a Happy New Year Xmas 1920

Georgina Maud Payne From Joe

All Alone Again
Joe Payne, British Home Child

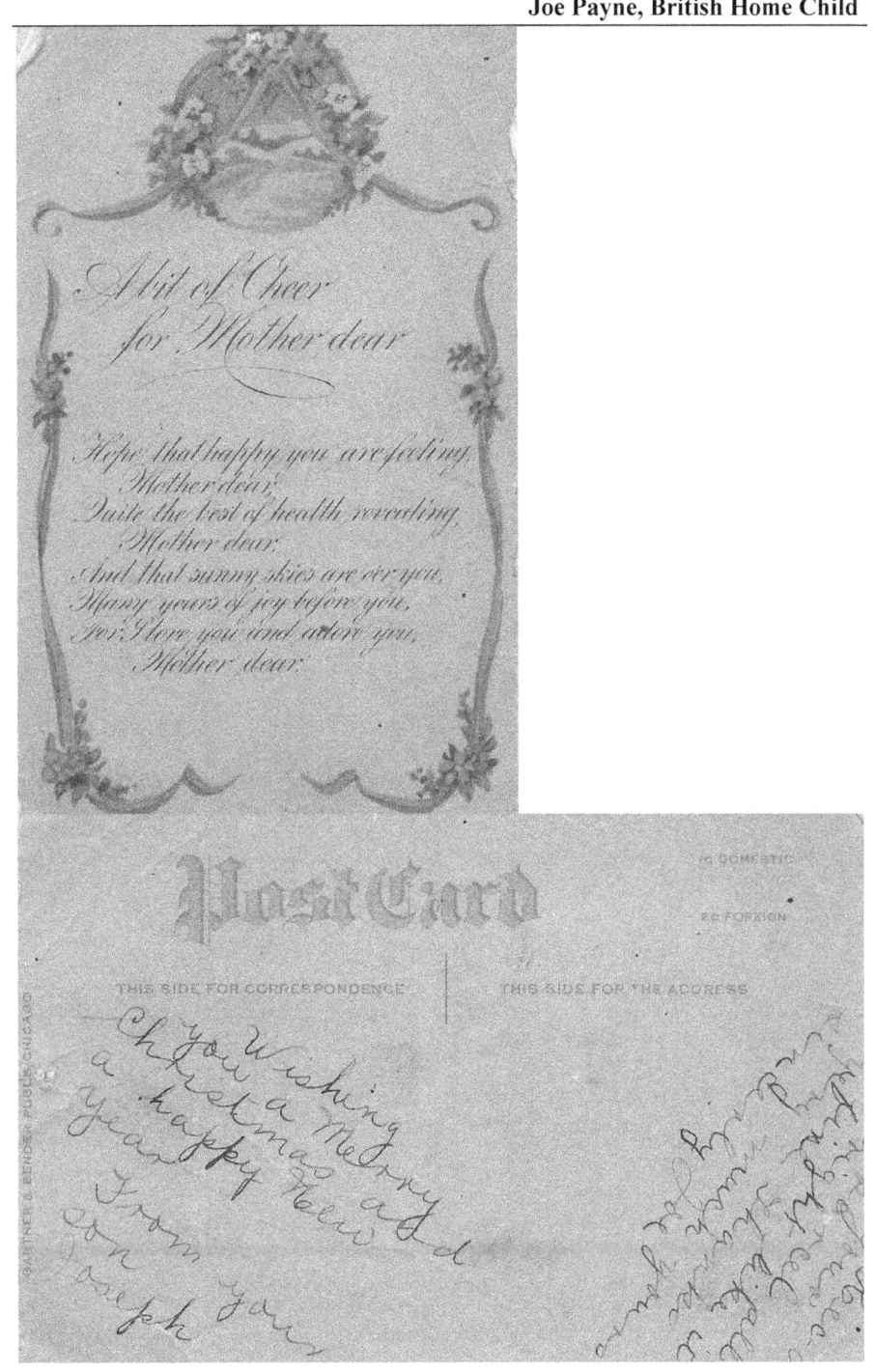

*A bit of Cheer
for Mother dear*

Hope that happy you are feeling,
 Mother dear;
Quite the best of health receding,
 Mother dear;
And that sunny skies are o'er you,
Many years of joy before you,
For I love you and adore you,
 Mother dear.

Post Card

Wishing you
a Merry Christmas and
a happy New
Year
From
son
Joseph

Carolyn MacIsaac

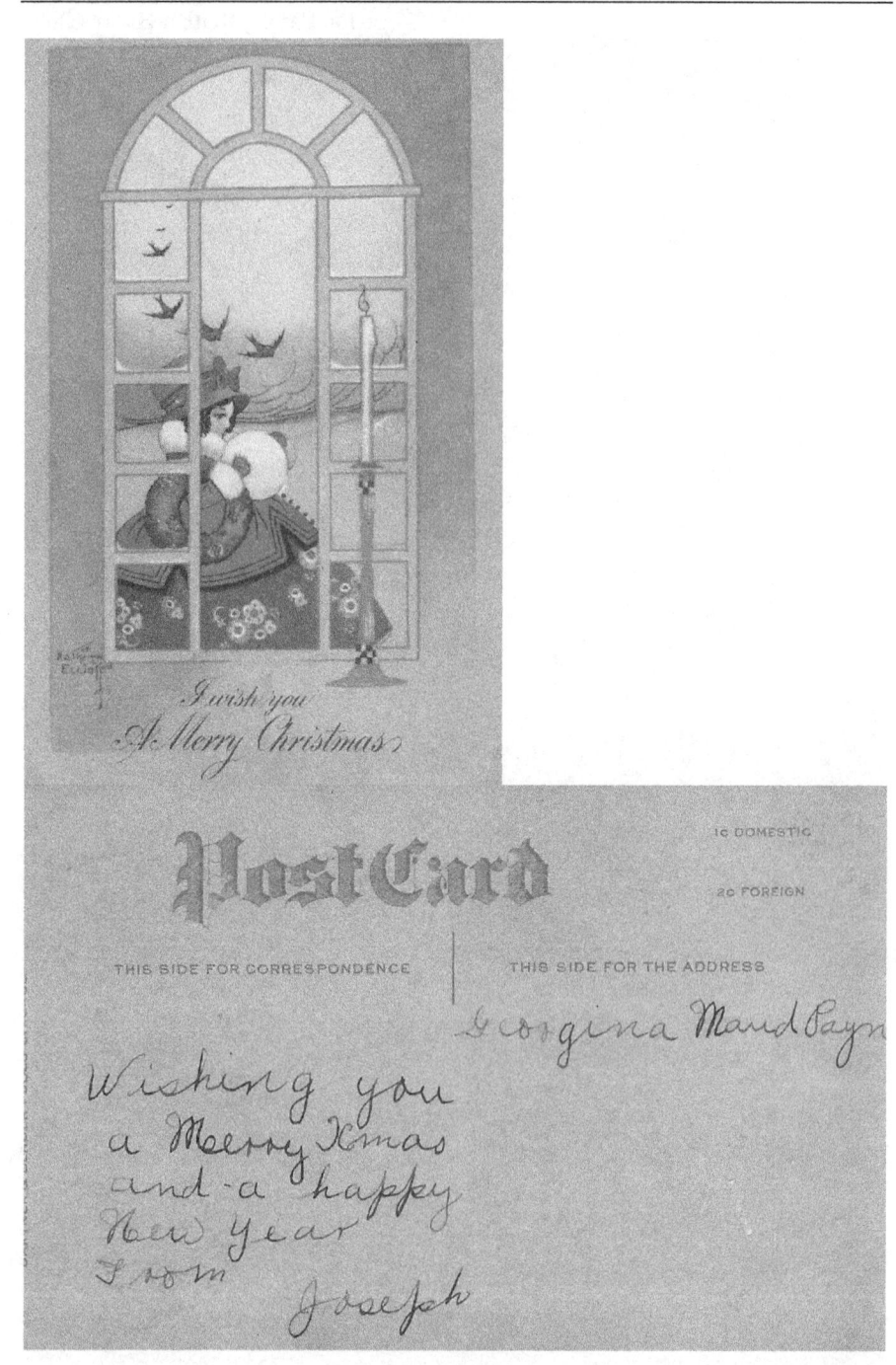

I wish you A Merry Christmas

Wishing you a Merry Xmas and a happy New Year from Joseph

Georgina Maud Payn

All Alone Again
Joe Payne, British Home Child

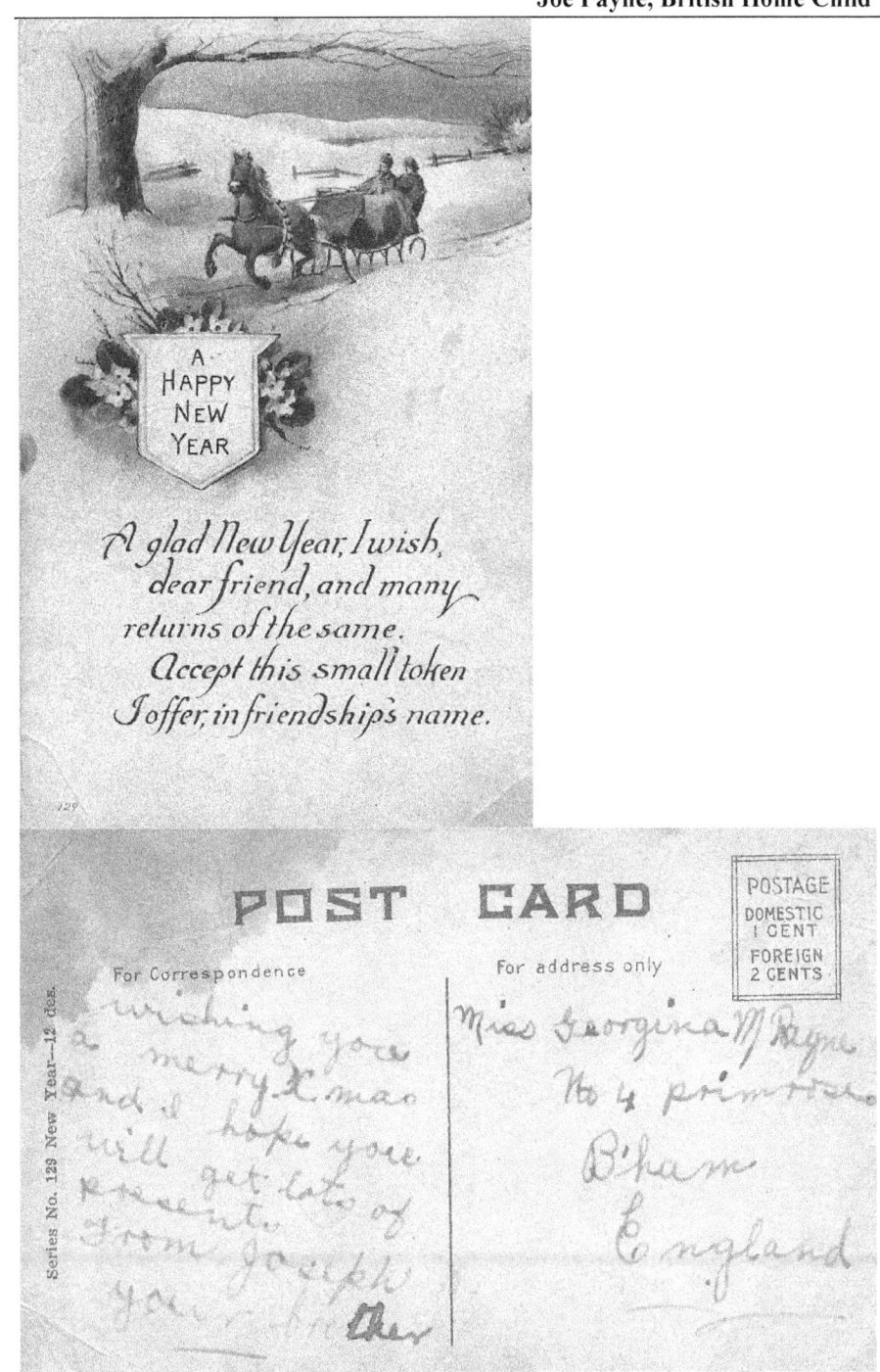

A glad New Year, I wish,
dear friend, and many
returns of the same.
Accept this small token
I offer, in friendship's name.

wishing you a merry Xmas and I hope you will get lots of presents. From Joseph your brother

Miss Georgina M Payne
No 4 prim...
B'ham
England

Carolyn MacIsaac

A Happy New Year
Good luck, Good health,
Good friends, Some wealth,
What can I wish you more
Than that the coming year may
Be more blest than all before.

Dec. 1923
I hope you will have a happy Xmas

Joseph

Miss Georgina M'Bryn
No 4 Primrose Ter
Heath St
Winson Green
Birmingham
Eng

All Alone Again
Joe Payne, British Home Child

Besides postcards, Joe's mother also tried to send him gifts when she could. One cold, snowy February evening, in 1920, when the children went for the mail, there was a package for Joe. He was excited. It wasn't Christmas or his birthday. He tore off his mitts and carefully cut the string off the brown paper wrapped package. His mum had sent him a book. It was titled "The Bell in The Forest." Inside the front cover was written, Dear Joe…with Mother's fond love…14/1/1920. One can only imagine the emotions the mother felt as she bought, wrapped and mailed this little book to her son who was growing up in a foreign land. Did he understand? Did he ever guess how it had ripped her heart out to lose him?

The years Alice had spent in Birmingham were terrible. Besides her poor health, long working hours and horrible living conditions there had also been the air raids and fear of war. One time she saw a German Zeppelin drop a bomb on the north side of Birmingham.

After the war had ended, Josiah had returned to Blockley. For whatever reason, he never tried to find his wife and daughter in Birmingham. He had heard what happened to Joe. The war had taken its toll on him. He had spent years in the damp, smelly, rat infested trenches that were meant to be a shelter and protection from the enemy. There had been constant fear of an attack from the enemy, besides a strong chance of catching typhoid fever, cholera or trench foot.

One night while Josiah had been drinking cider at the local pub, what started as an argument ended up in a bar fight. Someone had a gun, and Josiah lost an eye. It was considered a shooting accident. Lady Churchill, Captain Edward Spencer Churchill's mother had taken over the Northwick estate after Lady Northwick had died. Lady Churchill was fond of Josiah and paid for him to travel to London to see a top specialist on Harley Street. However, the specialist was unable to save the eye.

When the war was over, Alice had continued to work at Nettlefolds in Birmingham, making metal clips, hooks and fasteners for baby prams. Since the factory was on Heath Street she was able to find a place to live closer to her work at Number 4, Primrose Terrace on Heath Street, Winston Green. Living nearer her work saved her money since she didn't have to travel on the tram to get to and from work.

How she missed Joe. What was he doing? How was he doing? She was managing now. She didn't have enough money to send for him, but even if she had, Joe was lost to her forever. She had been persuaded to sign papers for him, to not only go to Canada, but he was under contract to work for the MacInnis family until he was eighteen. No, it was impossible for him to come back to England. There was never a day went by though, that she didn't think of him. She had sent him many cards over the years, and she would send him a little gift when she could. Canada was a huge wilderness. They probably didn't have books. She would send him some reading material from time to time.

Joe was to find out many years later that his mother thought Canada was a great wilderness without stores that sold books.

Walking back home, Joe held the parcel under his coat to keep it dry. The book was something new to add to his keepsakes. He would never guess, that a hundred years from now, he would have a daughter who would treasure the book in her collection.

That June and the following June in 1921, it was Robert Plenderleith who visited from Middlemore Emigration Home in Halifax. In 1920, he found Joe doing good and in grade 8 at school. In 1921, Robert didn't see Joe as he was working away at a Sawmill. Joe was still only receiving board and clothing in lieu of wages and he attended school only in winter. His health was good except that he suffered from occasional headaches. Mrs. MacInnis commented that Joe was not always truthful or honest but they would not like to be without him now. One must remember that in Joe's childhood in England he had stolen a drink of milk in order to survive. Mrs. MacInnis also mentioned that Joe heard regularly from his mother. His mother's love from afar helped Joe grow into a responsible adult. It was rare for a British Home Child to have that connection with a parent back in England.

Over the next few years, the girls left home one at a time as they moved away to find work. Jessie and Christina were the first to leave in 1920. Jessie went to her sister Mary Sarah's in Truro and Christina moved to Boston in the USA. A year later Mary Christine and Hughena joined Christina in Boston. Joe missed them. Sometimes

All Alone Again
Joe Payne, British Home Child

he would receive a postcard from one of them at Christmas or on his birthday. These cards he would put in his scrapbook with the ones from England.

81

Carolyn MacIsaac

All Alone Again
Joe Payne, British Home Child

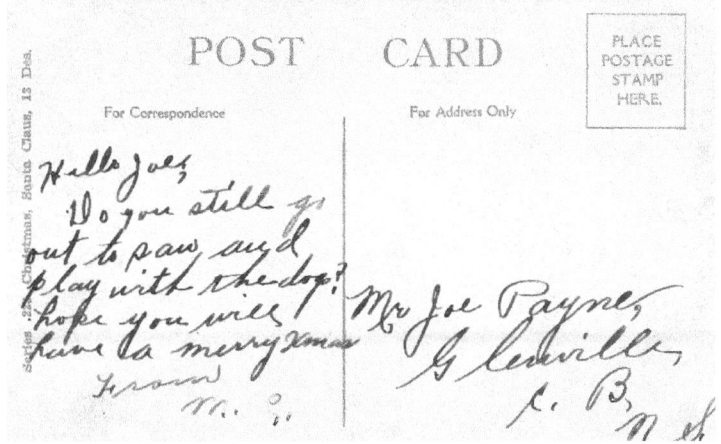

Carolyn MacIsaac

Forget that on roses
    thorns must grow,
Forget that shadows are
    made by a glow.
Forget your own ills
and remember that you,
In forgetting these things,
    are worthily true.
            J.G.S.

POST CARD

Master Joseph Payne,
Glenville,
Inverness,
Cape Breton

All Alone Again
Joe Payne, British Home Child

Carolyn MacIsaac

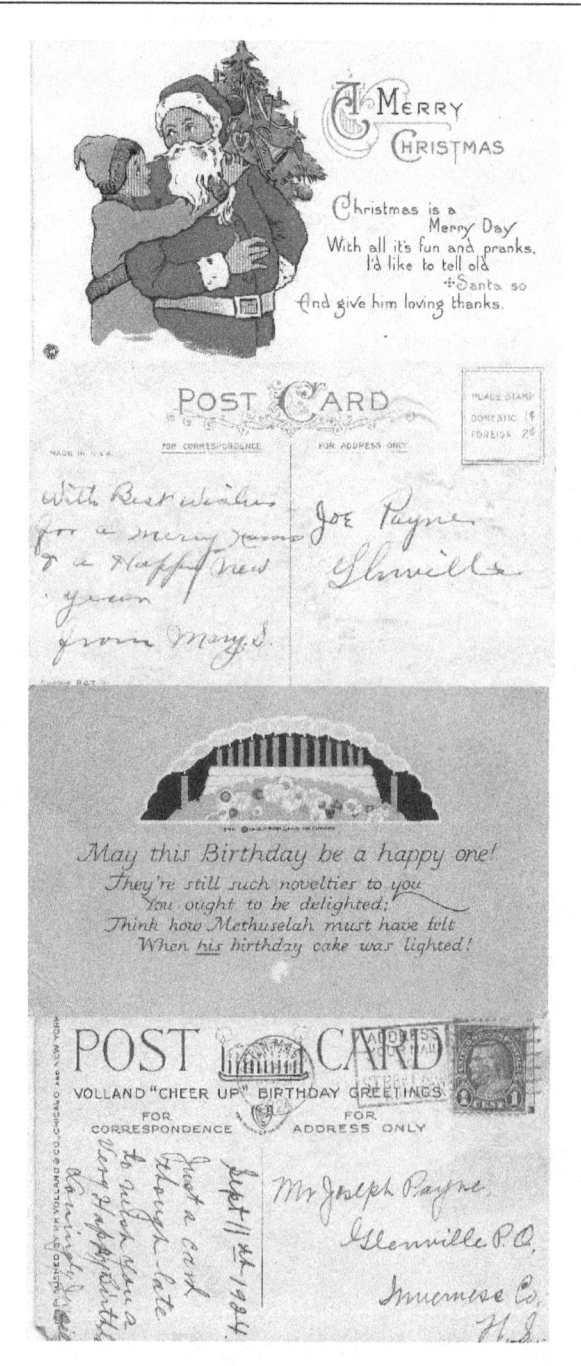

A Merry Christmas

Christmas is a Merry Day
With all it's fun and pranks.
I'd like to tell old
   ⁕Santa so
And give him loving thanks.

POST CARD

With Best wishes
for a merry xmas
& a Happy New
year
from Mary S.

Joe Payne
Glenville

May this Birthday be a happy one!
They're still such novelties to you
You ought to be delighted;
Think how Methuselah must have felt
When *his* birthday cake was lighted!

POST CARD — VOLLAND "CHEER UP" BIRTHDAY GREETINGS

Sept 11th 1924.

Just a card
though late
to wish you a
Very Happy Birthday

Mr Joseph Payne,
Glenville P.O.,
Inverness Co.
N.S.

All Alone Again
Joe Payne, British Home Child

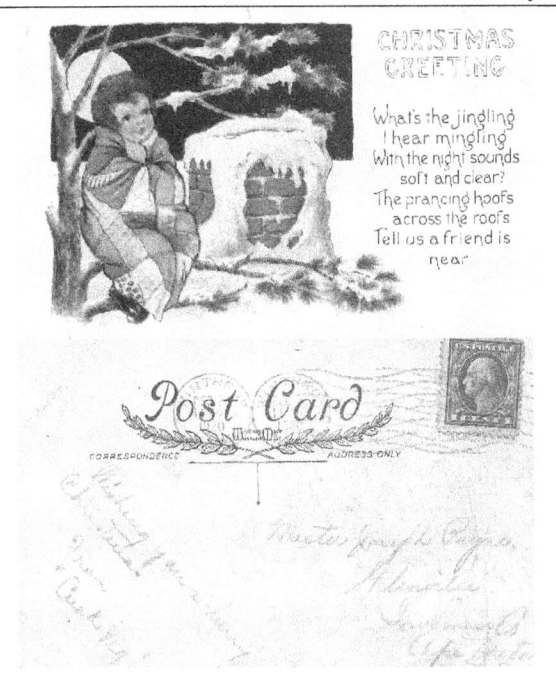

Carolyn MacIsaac

All Alone Again
Joe Payne, British Home Child

Carolyn MacIsaac

All Alone Again
Joe Payne, British Home Child

Carolyn MacIsaac

All Alone Again
Joe Payne, British Home Child

93

Carolyn MacIsaac

THIS IS MY MESSAGE
TO YOU —
EASTER JOY, GOOD WISHES
TOO!

Post Card

Easter Greetings,
From
Mary C.

Master Joe Payne,
Glenville,
C. B,
N.S.

Chapter 7

Joseph Payne (1920 – 1932)
Finding Work

Joe

Joe dreamed of the day that he would turn eighteen and also leave the farm. Where would he go? Mary Sarah, the oldest MacInnis girl was married and living in Truro on the mainland of Nova Scotia. He had gotten to know Mary Sarah and her children Allan and Malcolm and her step-son Silas when they visited the farm every summer. Joe had also traveled through Truro on the train when he was nine and had first arrived in Canada. Perhaps he would go and stay with Mary Sarah for a few days until he found work. He knew farming, working in the woods cutting down trees and other odd jobs he had learned throughout the years. He knew how to build things and he was really good at math. The little schooling he had, he excelled at.

The summer Joe was to turn eighteen the household was down to just five; Ma MacInnis, Neil, Aleana, Clifford and Joe. Jessie had left Truro and joined her sisters in Boston. Joe was torn between feeling needed at the farm and wanting to get away from it. Although he was no longer under contract to work for the MacInnis family, he remained on the farm for one more year.

Mr. Ray had visited Joe in August of 1922 and for the last time in August of 1923. He wrote on the report that everything was fair except that Joe was small for his age. He was now receiving spending money along with his board and clothing. Mr. Ray wrote.

Joe will start on his own after the close of the farming season – he is now an able bodied youth, and should be quite easily capable of taking care of himself.

Joe had no desire to return to England, although he continued to send and receive cards from his mum and Ena. His father, Josiah, passed away in a workhouse in Shipston on Stour on January 18, 1924. It was a sad end to Josiah's life. The workhouse provided food and shelter for the poor and elderly who were unable to support themselves, but the conditions were horrific and they were often referred to as a death trap. It was much like a prison with bare crowded rooms, poor nutrition and no games or books. The buildings built to hold 700 people often had 5000 or more crowded into them. The men were given work to do, unravelling rope or crushing stone. People died every day and were often buried along the wall of the workhouse. Joe was never told of his father's death. He always believed he had gone missing in the war.

Joe was nineteen when he finally asked Mary Sarah if he could travel back to Truro with her family. She had been home with her children for a visit. Joe had formed a friendship with her step-son Silas over the years. They sometimes sent postcards to each other.

Silas had written, "Come visit us."

Joe had written back, "Perhaps I will go back with you the next time you visit."

All Alone Again
Joe Payne, British Home Child

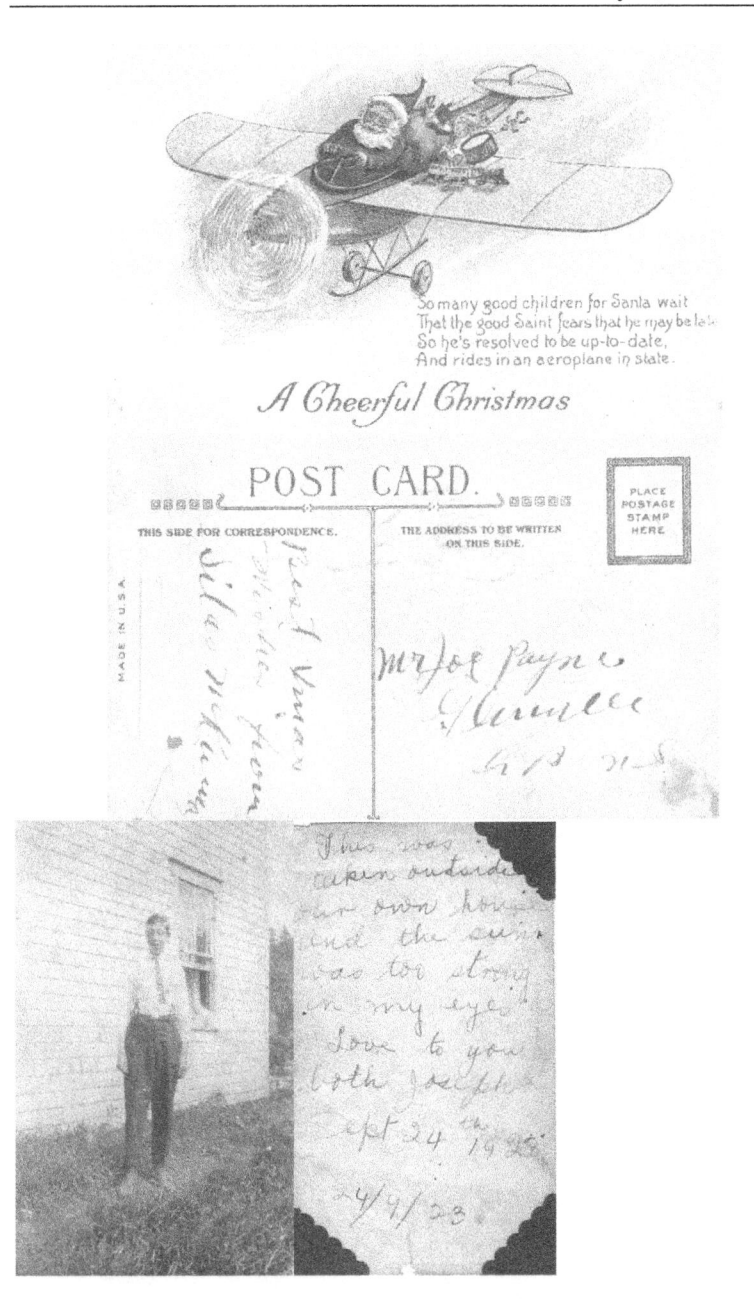

Carolyn MacIsaac

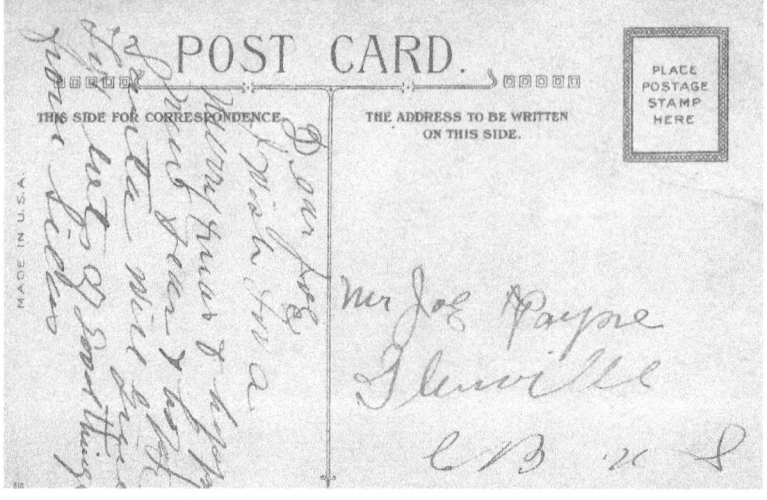

All Alone Again
Joe Payne, British Home Child

    Mary Sarah encouraged him to leave the farm and find a job on the mainland. She told him they could offer him a bed for a few days until he found work.

    And so, Joe finally packed his few belongings, and against Ma's wishes, he said good-bye to the MacInnis family and was on his way. He never looked back. He didn't intend to ever go back. Joe stayed with the MacKinnon family briefly while looking for a job. Ma sent him a letter telling him she missed him and asked him to come back to the farm if he couldn't find work.

A Merry Christmas & A Happy New Year to You

Post Card

dear Joe how are you getting along we all miss you a lot and if you cannot get work dont hesitate to come back any day you feel like it good bye from ma

Mr Joe Payne
Truro
N S

Carolyn MacIsaac

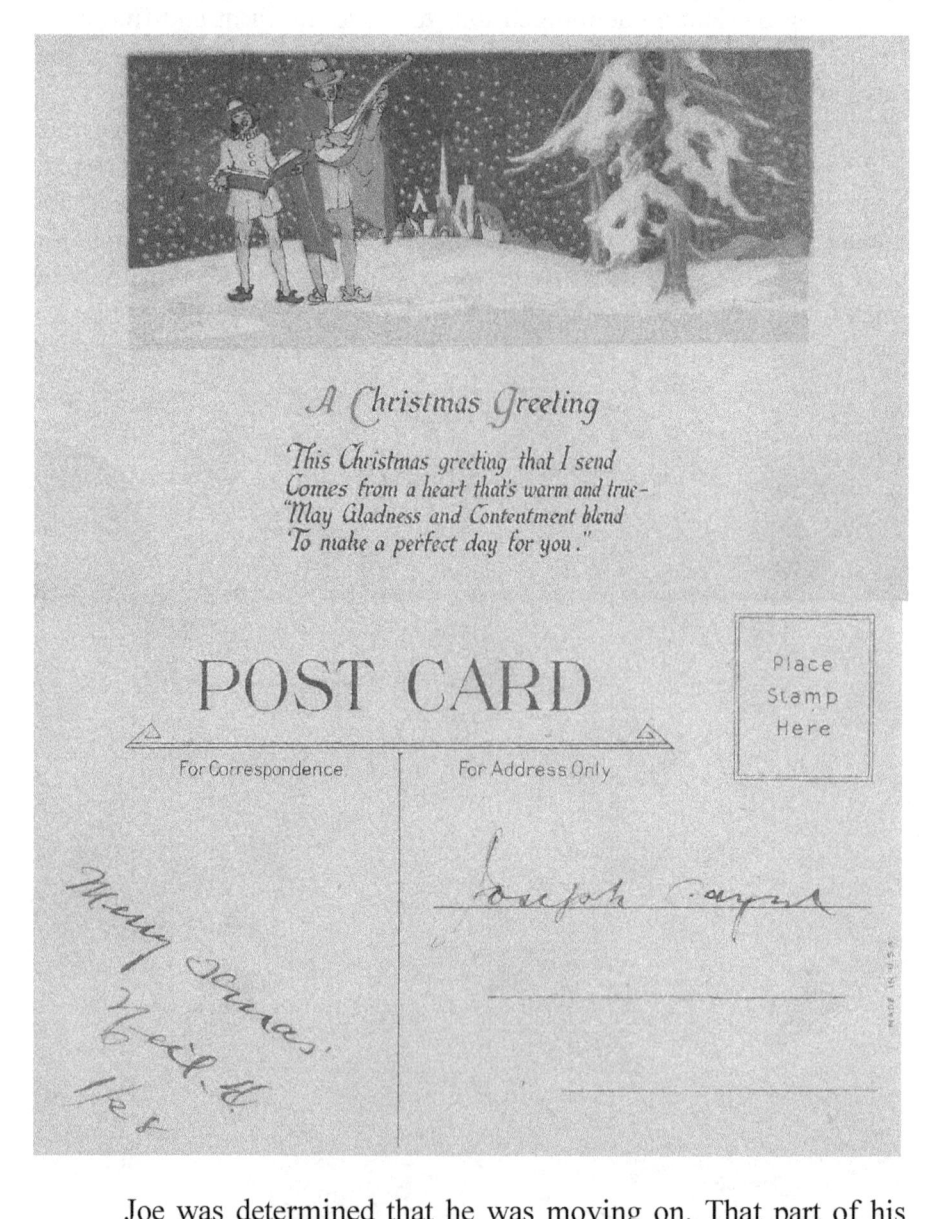

Joe was determined that he was moving on. That part of his life, where he was indentured, was over. His first job was working on a farm in Nuttby, about fifteen miles north of Truro. The work in Nuttby was too much like the farm work he had left behind in Glenville. While there he heard talk of a harvest train going to

All Alone Again
Joe Payne, British Home Child

western Canada. Evidently, every summer farmers in western Canada needed thousands of seasonal workers to harvest the wheat.

It was to the railway's benefit to lower the price of a train ticket to half price since they made money exporting the wheat. By August of 1926, Joe had saved the money to buy a ticket and got on the train in Truro with a large group of men and headed out west. There was a policeman onboard to keep the men from too much rowdiness. The week-long journey was spent sitting on hard wooden seats, playing cards and listening to music. There were countless stops along the way as more harvesters were picked up. Some stops would be long enough for Joe to get off the train to buy a bite of food.

Joe was introduced to cigarettes on the trip out west. Although he tried several times over the years, he was never able to beat the addiction. He was also offered liquor but he never drank.

Joe traveled all the way to Tugask, Saskatchewan, farming country a little northwest of Moose Jaw, before he found work. There he worked hard for sixteen hours a day from dawn to dusk, a job that defeated many. For the first week, the workers picked rocks until the harvest was ready. He had been used to hard work on the farm in Glenville so he survived. Many of the men who went out on the harvest train got a grant of land and stayed in the prairies, but when Joe had been there for two months and the harvesters were no longer needed that fall, he headed back to Nova Scotia. Nova Scotia had become home. He preferred the mountains and the valleys to the flat land in the prairie provinces of Canada where all you could see were fields of wheat when you looked in any direction.

Over the next several years, Joe changed jobs from farming to working in lumber camps. He worked in River Hebert, Cumberland County, one winter and Caledonia, Guysborough County, the next. In 1928, he became a tallyman in the woods in Merigomish.

The camps were all about the same. Some had only one bunkhouse, and some had three. The beds, often infested with bedbugs, were all crowded together in one building with a potbellied stove in the center. They would be awake at five in the morning and go to a building next door where the cook prepared the meals. The rough wood table was long and centered in the room. Here they ate their breakfast and took a lunch to eat in the woods.

Carolyn MacIsaac

Once in the woods, trees would be selected to harvest. Usually spruce, pine and fir were cut leaving the maple, oak, birch and other hardwood trees for special orders. The larger, better trees were designated for lumber, and the smaller, crooked trees were separated for pulp. Two men working together would cut down a tree using a crosscut saw. The tree was then cut to a certain length, and the limbs would be removed with an axe. Sometimes the bark was left on the pulpwood. However, the wood was worth more with the bark removed. The pulpwood was cut to four-foot lengths and stacked in piles four feet high, four feet wide and eight feet long. Each pile was a cord. The pulpwood was then hauled to the railway station. Here it was loaded on a railway car and shipped to a pulp mill where the wood would eventually be transformed into paper.

On site, the tallymen, using a ruler and calipers would measure the diameter of the tree in inches, and estimate the market value of the logs being sent to the mill. This would be recorded on a tally board. On one side would be a list of possible diameters and on the other side, a tally would be marked with logs matching that diameter. The tallymen would also estimate how many board feet were in each log and write it on the end of the log.

The better logs used for lumber would be cut thirteen feet in length. A team of oxen would take the logs on a skid to the mill where the logs were made into lumber.

A sawyer at the mill would decide which way was best to cut each log individually for size and use. Slabs were cut off all four sides leaving a rectangular timber. The timber was then dried and planed.

After a long day in the woods, the men returned to the camp for supper. In the evening some men would sit around the fire and play cards while others knit warm wool socks to keep their feet warm. One man by the name of Buddy sat and carved animals from wood. Joe took an interest in wood carving, and Buddy helped him carve a beautiful horse. When it was finished he rubbed linseed oil into the wood. The horse was an accomplishment, and Joe treasured it. Someday he would have a mantle in a house that he had built himself and be able to display it.

All Alone Again
Joe Payne, British Home Child

Joe had been at the lumber camp in Merigomish for a couple months when the men went home for Christmas. Joe returned to his rented room in Truro. The snow was too deep that winter to do any logging, so it was March before Joe and the other men returned to the camp. When one tallyman didn't return after the winter break, Joe jumped at the chance to take over his job measuring and counting the logs. Joe was good with figures, and he was given the job over other men who couldn't read or write.

It was a cold job. No matter how many layers of long-johns Joe wore, the cold dampness still crept into his skinny bones. At six foot he was still a very slim man.

The last two MacInnis girls, Hughena and Alena had joined their sisters in Boston. Neil and Clifford remained with Ma MacInnis on the farm. Christy's brother, Uncle Fred and her sister, Christy Ann, who was deaf, also came to live with them for the remainder of their lives. In the 1920's it was a trend for families to take in their elderly parents and aunts and uncles with no children of their own to look after them.

Joe never saw Ma MacInnis again, but he did receive postcards and letters from Ma and Neil and the girls in Boston. Only two of the girls, Jessie and Hughena returned to Cape Breton, got married and raised their families in Inverness County. The other three, Alena, Christina and Mary Christine married and raised their families in the United States.

John Middlemore, founder of Middlemore Emigration Homes, had died on October 17, 1925. Mr. Ray died in 1931 at the age of 55. He had spent 41 years in Canada and 17 years in office.

Joe met many young girls over the years. He got Christmas cards and letters from Una in Saskatchewan and from Myrtle and

Carolyn MacIsaac

Annie in Nova Scotia. He had Betty's ring. But, none of them was the girl.

All Alone Again
Joe Payne, British Home Child

105

Carolyn MacIsaac

All Alone Again
Joe Payne, British Home Child

A Merry Christmas

With all kind thoughts and good wishes for Christmas and the New Year.

Christmas 1924

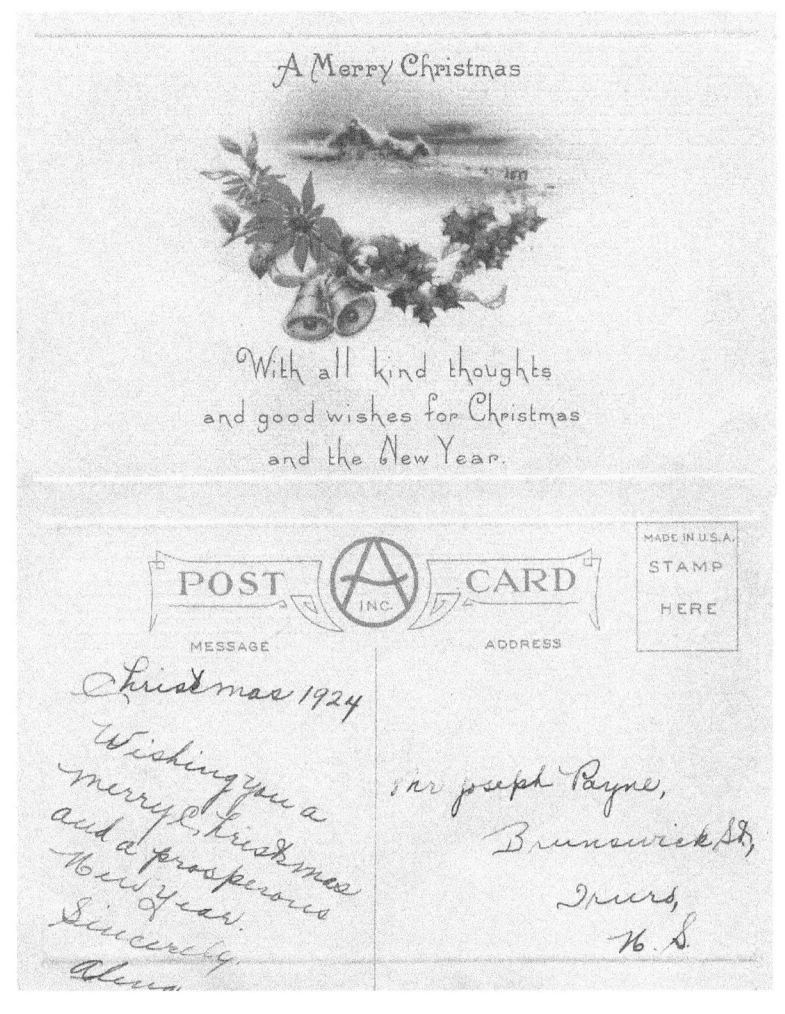

Wishing you a merry Christmas and a prosperous New Year. Sincerely, Alma

Mr Joseph Payne,
Brunswick St,
Truro,
N.S.

Horse Joe carved

Carolyn MacIsaac

Joe also continued to get cards from England.

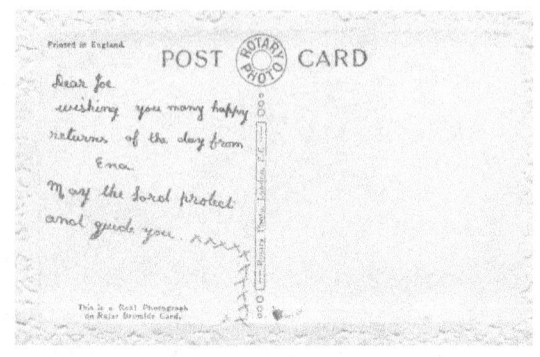

108

All Alone Again
Joe Payne, British Home Child

To Greet My Son's Birthday

Upon this day I greet you
With wishes fond and true
May all good fortune meet you
That lasts your whole life through

POST CARD

Dearest Joe
with love &
best wishes
from Mother.
x x x x x x x x x

ADDRESS only to be here

This is a real photograph

Carolyn MacIsaac

All Alone Again
Joe Payne, British Home Child

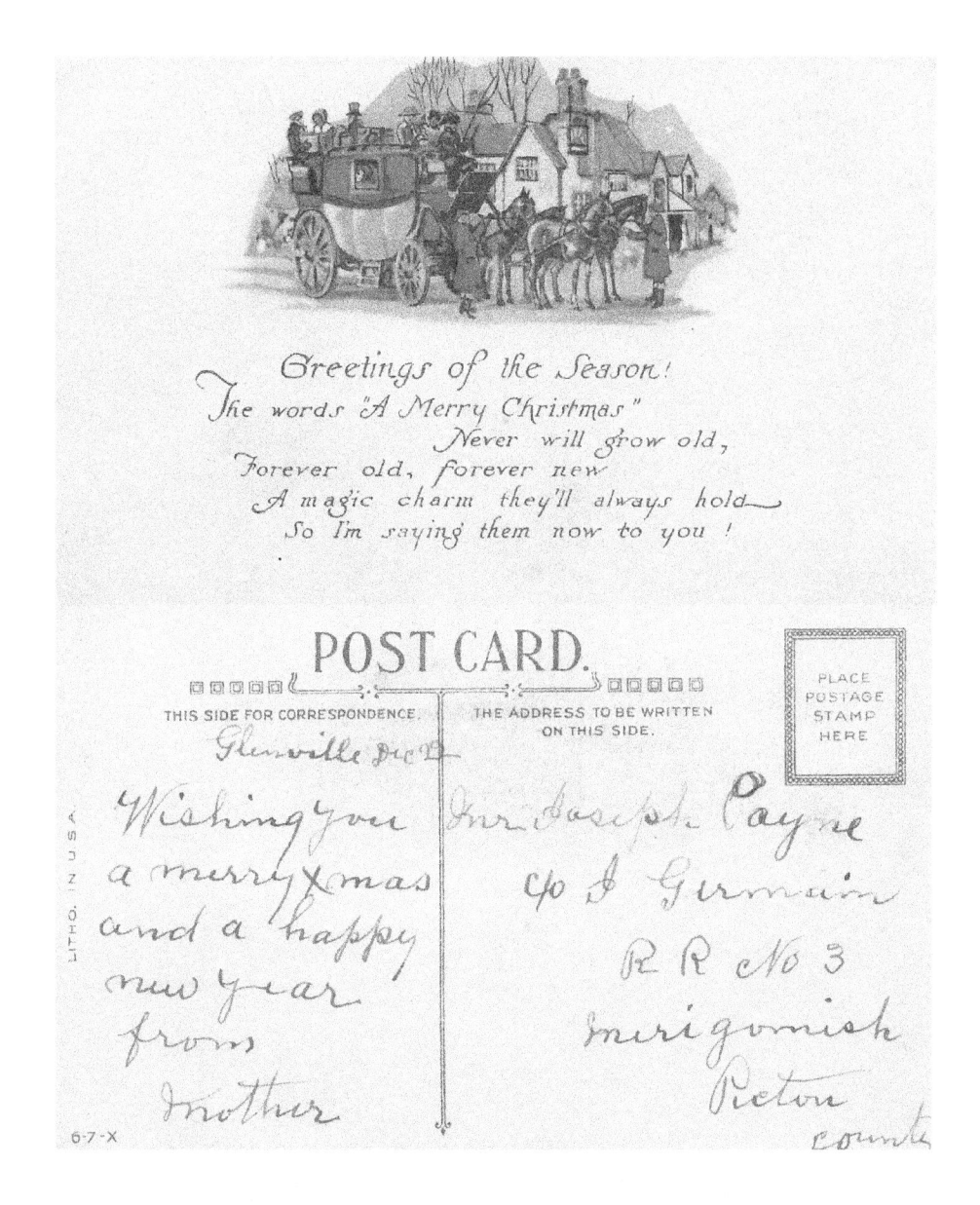

Greetings of the Season!
The words "A Merry Christmas"
        Never will grow old,
Forever old, forever new
A magic charm they'll always hold
So I'm saying them now to you!

POST CARD.

THIS SIDE FOR CORRESPONDENCE. | THE ADDRESS TO BE WRITTEN ON THIS SIDE.

Glenville Dec

Wishing you
a merry Xmas
and a happy
new year
from
Mother

Mr Joseph Payne
c/o I Germain
R R No 3
Merigomish
Picton
county

111

Carolyn MacIsaac

Many Happy Returns of your Birthday

DEAR SON

BIRTHDAY Greetings
TO WISH YOU
every HAPPINESS

With
Sincere Greetings and
all Good Wishes on
your Birthday;
May you be blessed
with every Happiness,
and may the future
bring you Health and
and Better Times.

dear Joe with all my love &
best wishes from Mother

All Alone Again
Joe Payne, British Home Child

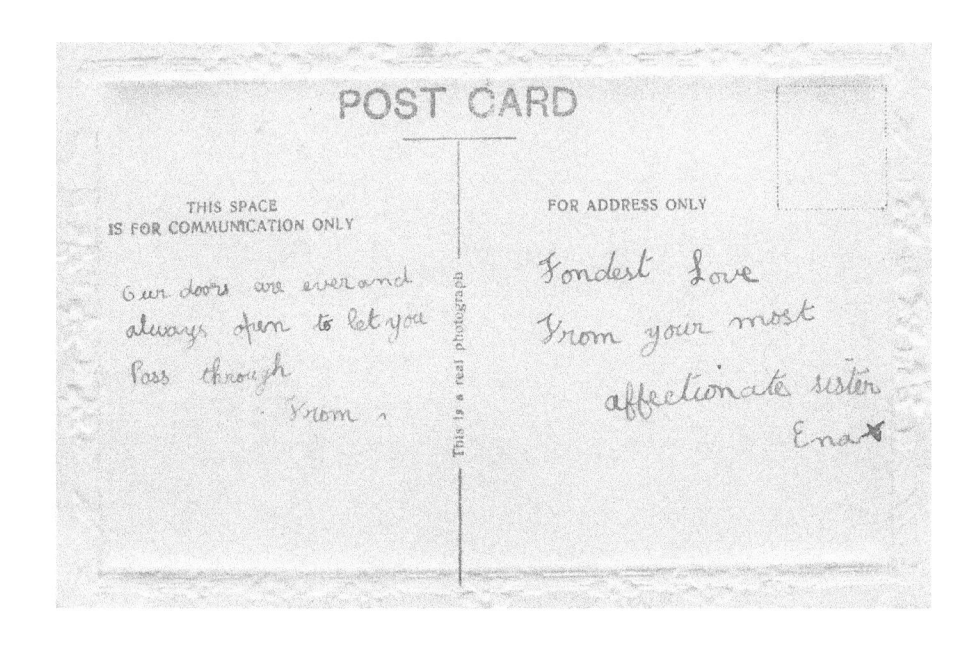

To my BROTHER on his BIRTHDAY

Within your heart may joys abide,
Good fortune all your actions bless,
The doors of love be open wide
To welcome you with happiness.

POST CARD

THIS SPACE IS FOR COMMUNICATION ONLY

Our doors are ever and always open to let you pass through
· From ·

FOR ADDRESS ONLY

Fondest Love
From your most affectionate sister
Ena

113

Carolyn MacIsaac

All Alone Again
Joe Payne, British Home Child

To my BROTHER on his Birthday

This greeting which I send to you to-day
Has kindest thoughts to speed it on its way
And brings a wish that all the future through
Life will hold nought but happiness for you

POST CARD

THIS SPACE IS FOR COMMUNICATION ONLY

FOR ADDRESS ONLY

Fondest Wishes from Ena & Les

Carolyn MacIsaac

Joyous Greetings from Over the Sea

Christmas bells are ringing
Gaily far and wide,
Hearts are re-united
Tho' oceans may divide. —
Happy time of Christmas!
May it bring to you
Happiness in plenty,
Love sincere and true.
E. Hutchings

To bring you
sweet recollections
and many wishes for
Christmas
and
New Year happiness.

From Ena to my dear
brother with greatest love xxx

All Alone Again
Joe Payne, British Home Child

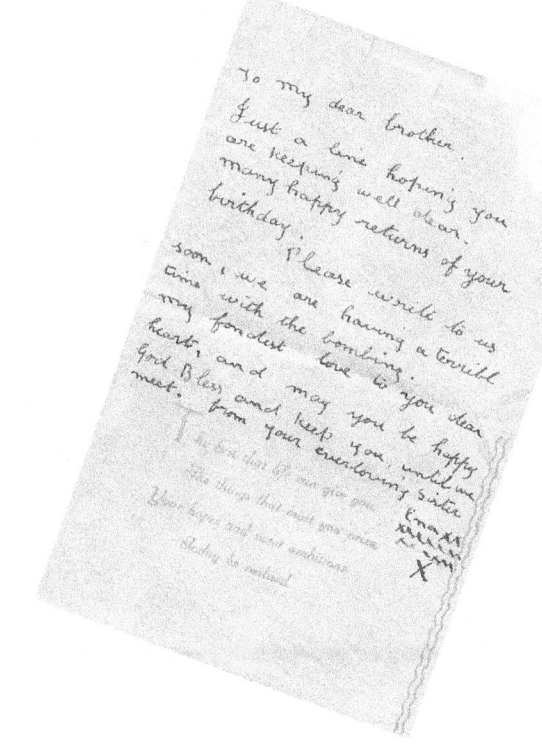

A Happy Birthday to my Dear Brother

To my dear brother,
Just a line hoping you are keeping well dear. Many happy returns of your birthday. Please write to us soon. We are having a terrible time with the bombing. My fondest love to you dear heart, and may you be happy. God bless and keep you, until we meet.
From your everloving sister,
    X

Carolyn MacIsaac

This card wasn't signed

Chapter 8

Ola
Truro, Nova Scotia (1932 – 1945)

Walking down Brunswick Street, just a few steps in front of him, was a tiny young woman who seemed to be struggling with two bags of what Joe assumed were heavy groceries. He followed slowly.

When she stopped to move things around in her arms, Joe caught up to her.

Carolyn MacIsaac

"You look like you could use some help," he offered.

She looked up at him with the most beautiful brown eyes Joe had ever seen. They were the darkest brown. Her face, framed by soft, curly, light brown hair, lit up with the brightest smile imaginable.

Joe towered almost a foot above her.

"I thought my sister was going to meet me to help carry them," she said.

"Here, let me help" Joe offered.

"That's okay," she replied, "I just live, not very far up, on this next street."

The next street was Young Street, and it was quite steep. She would be turning off to the right. Joe was living on Wood Street just off Brunswick Street, a few streets up on the left. Nevertheless, he fully intended to help this young maiden with her parcels.

"I am going that way myself," Joe lied. He reached out for one bag, and Ola let him take it.

"My Name is Joe Payne…and yours?"

"Ola, Ola Sharpe."

"Mrs. Sharpe?" he asked, trying to see if she wore a wedding ring.

"No, I'm not married. I live just up ahead on the left, with my mother and father, my brother, and five of my sisters."

As they arrived at 125 Young Street, two young girls came running out.

There is a new Bungalow at 125 Young Street today, but Ola's parent's house was identical to the one on the left.

"I'm sorry. I got busy, and forgot I was supposed to meet you," one of the girls exclaimed. "Who is this?" she said with a giggle.

"Ola took the bag from Joe and handed it to one of the girls. Then she quickly turned to Joe, said thanks, and hurried towards the house.

Joe could hear one of the girls singing, "Ollie has a boyfriend."

"I wish," he thought. He didn't know if he would see her again, but he wanted to. He continued walking up Young Street, took a shortcut down into the park, and eventually found his way back to Brunswick Street. Tired at the end of the day, he somehow had a lighter step.

Joe returned to the lumber camp the next day. Over the next couple of weeks, Ola was often on his mind. Every time he was back in Truro he would watch for her, hoping to catch her walking home from work alone. It was a couple of months before he finally came across her walking with three of her sisters. Ola introduced him to

Carolyn MacIsaac

Lillie, Vernie and Jennie. The sisters had of course heard about Joe, and although curious, they allowed their sister to step back and walk alone with him. Joe and Ola strolled more slowly than the others, and Joe told her a bit about himself, that he worked as a tallyman in the woods and had a room on Wood Street when he wasn't at camp. Ola told him she was walking home from her job at Lewis Ltd. where they made hats. Ola and the three sisters she was walking with worked at the factory. They lived at home with their parents and paid board money. Joe walked her home, and just before they reached her driveway, in case her younger sisters came running out again, he asked if she would go to the pictures with him. There was a Greta Garbo movie playing that he thought she would enjoy.

Saturday evening, he knocked on her door as planned. One of the younger sisters answered the door, and led him into the kitchen. She told Joe her name was Edith, and she introduced him to her mother and father.

There wasn't much money for eating out or going to the pictures, so whenever Joe was not at camp, he and Ola spent a lot of time with her family. Besides the two younger sisters and the three he had met walking her home from work, Ola had four more sisters and two brothers. The three younger ones were still in school. Her oldest sister, Margaret, was married and living just up on Brunswick Street. Her sisters, Prudence and Lahlia, were married, and residing just outside the town of Truro. She also had an older brother Lawrence, married and living further up on Young Street, on another property her father had once owned.

Ola had many nieces and nephews. Often on a day off work, when Joe was home from camp, she and Joe would take the children to the beautiful Victoria Park in Truro. Ola and Joe would push the children on the swings, and sometimes, they would sit on a swing with a toddler on their lap.

On a nice evening, Ola and Joe would go for a walk in the park. There was usually at least one sister with them.

Through time Joe told Ola a little more about himself. "I was put in an orphanage in England when I was barely nine years old. Even though my parents were alive, the authorities didn't think they were able to provide for me. I guess, times were hard for them. When

All Alone Again
Joe Payne, British Home Child

my father went to war, and my mother needed an operation, she had no other choice."

Ola slowly shook her head with a sad look on her face.

Joe continued to tell her, "I did have my mother's address so that I could write to her. I receive letters and presents from her on my birthday and at Christmastime. As a skinny little nine-year-old, I crossed the Atlantic Ocean on a ship and spent the next ten years working on a farm in Cape Breton. As soon as I turned eighteen, I had wanted to leave the farm, but remained another year before I found work on the mainland." Joe then told her, about traveling out west to work on the wheat farms during harvest time. "And, I didn't care for the flat countryside, so I came back to Nova Scotia. Mary Sarah, one of the daughters of the people I worked for in Cape Breton is married with two children. She lives not too far from here on Brunswick Street. I stayed with them until I found a job and a place of my own. Truro is my home now."

Ola told Joe that she had been born in Renfrew Mines, but didn't live there long as her parents moved around a lot. Her father, Charles, farmed in the summer, and they moved to town for most winters where he found work as a foreman for the Truro town works. "We have lived in Shubenacadie, Londonderry, and Truro. Since we have moved here, we have lived on Willow Street, East Prince Street, Arthur Street, and Brunswick Street, before we moved to the house we now live in on Young Street. When my youngest sister, Lydia, was two, Papa bought the farm in Hilden. We used to move back there in late spring in time to get the garden planted. It is just a couple of miles further up on Young street. This year Papa sold the farm to my brother Lawrence. Lawrence and Blanche are expecting their second child."

Ola was the seventh child of thirteen. Two of her siblings had died in infancy.

"Life must have been hard for such a large family," Joe said.

"I guess it must have been, but we didn't know any different, and we were happy. We only wore shoes in the winter, and went barefoot in the summer."

"It must have been hard for your parents to feed such a large family let alone buy shoes for them."

Ola nodded. "My favorite meal is beef stew. We children always ate the broth over a piece of bread. Papa got the meat. We didn't mind. Broth on bread tastes wonderful. Have you tried it, Joe?"

"Yup, and I agree it tastes good. Have you ever had pap, warm milk poured over stale bread? That tastes great for breakfast too."

"With sugar on it, I presume?"

"Yes, brown sugar if you can get it."

There was a severe worldwide economic depression known as the Great Depression, in the 1930's. It was a result of the stock market crash in the 1920's, where people, living in a more prosperous time after the war, invested heavily in the stock market. When everyone tried to cash in stocks at the same time, the Stock Market crashed. Now, with low income and high prices, the government rationed food to try and stabilize the economy, and help put a little food on the tables of the poor. There were rations of sugar, eggs, butter, cheese, coffee and meat. Each person was given an allotted amount of coupons for food purchases. The depression was to last until the start of the Second World War in 1939.

Remembering how cold the farmhouse got in Cape Breton, Joe asked Ola if she found her house cold in winter. He told her, "One time when I wasn't much more than nine, the girls thought it would have to be warmer outside than in. They went outside in their bare feet, and ran around and around the house in the snow trying to get warm."

"Did it work?"

"I don't think so," he said with a chuckle, "but I think one of the older girls got them a warmed brick from the oven to warm their feet in bed."

"When it is really cold in the winter, we don't go outside to the toilet during the night. The pot we have a pee in during the night turns to ice by morning. My sisters and I have to take turns emptying it, and sometimes it is as hard as ice." She blushed a little and they both laughed.

"What about school?" Joe asked. He had only been able to attend school in winter when he wasn't needed at home to do farm work.

"None of us girls went to school beyond grade nine. We stopped when we reached puberty and stayed home and helped

All Alone Again
Joe Payne, British Home Child

Mama. Even when we were younger we used to stay home from school on washday to help her. And, of course, moving around all the time didn't help. I was very smart in school. I learned to recite many poems." And she went on to recite the epic poem Evangeline by Henry Wadsworth Longfellow; ending with:

> *"She was a woman now, with the heart and hopes of a woman. which, as the farmers believed, would load their orchards with apples; she, too, would bring to her husband's house delight and abundance, filling it full of love and the ruddy faces of children."*

Ola sighed. "Education was never deemed important for us girls. It was thought that we would get married and never work. But, look at me, an old maid!"

"Not for long," was all he said.

Ola pretended not to hear. "You must be pretty smart, Joe, to be a tallyman in the woods."

"I guess. I always did well in arithmetic."

"Did you ever dream you'd like to be better educated?"

"I guess the only thing I ever wanted to be was a carpenter. I love taking wood and building something with it. I also like drawing a picture of what I'm wanting to make and trying to figure out how much material I need."

"You will have to become a carpenter then Joe. It is possible, isn't it?"

"I hope so. For now, I am working in the lumber mill." He hesitated for a moment. "I am thankful for that. It's hard to find steady work. I hope things get better. Someday I hope to have some tools and a garage so that I can start making a table or some other small piece of furniture." He hesitated again for a moment, and turned to look at her. "I have always wanted to build my own house."

"It's wonderful to have dreams, Joe."

Ola told Joe she had a scary story to tell him. "One time we were walking home from school at lunchtime. We had to cross railroad tracks, and there was a train stopped on the tracks. We waited for some time, but we were hungry, and didn't have a lot of time before we had to go back to school. I crawled under the train to get to the other side."

"You did what? You could have been killed." He shivered a little.

"That's not the worst of it. My sisters and brothers told me I was going to be in big trouble, so I crawled back through to where they waited."

Joe put his arms around her, holding her close for a few minutes not saying anything.

Joe was often away to the lumber camp for months at a time, and they wrote many letters to each other. Each time he came home to Truro, they picked up where they had left off. Joe only had eyes for Ola, and Ola turned away any men interested in pursuing a relationship with her.

Ola and Joe were in love, and on May 11, 1933, they were married by the Justice of the Peace. It was on a Thursday evening. After a simple wedding ceremony, they went back to Ola's parent's home to show them their rings. Both wore a plain gold band. The younger children had been put to bed, and Ola went upstairs to show them her ring.

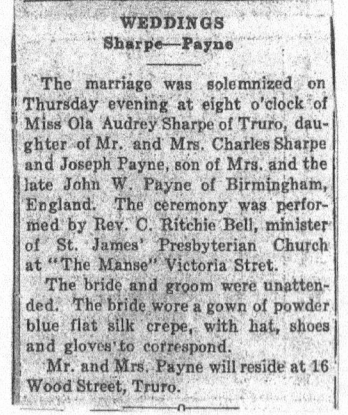

WEDDINGS
Sharpe—Payne

The marriage was solemnized on Thursday evening at eight o'clock of Miss Ola Audrey Sharpe of Truro, daughter of Mr. and Mrs. Charles Sharpe and Joseph Payne, son of Mrs. and the late John W. Payne of Birmingham, England. The ceremony was performed by Rev. C. Ritchie Bell, minister of St. James' Presbyterian Church at "The Manse" Victoria Street.

The bride and groom were unattended. The bride wore a gown of powder blue flat silk crepe, with hat, shoes and gloves to correspond.

Mr. and Mrs. Payne will reside at 16 Wood Street, Truro.

Joe's house on Wood Street

After many "oos" and "ahs" and "congratulations," Joe and Ola slipped away to Joe's home on Wood Street. For the first time in her twenty-five years, Ola would not be saying good-night to her parents

All Alone Again
Joe Payne, British Home Child

and siblings. Every night when they went to bed, they had started, from eldest to youngest, saying good-night to each other.

"Good-night Maggie."
"Good-night Ollie."
"Good-night Prudy."
"Good–night Ollie."

This would take at least ten minutes.

The one room Joe rented wasn't quite adequate for the newlyweds, so they soon found a larger house to rent, a little further out of town on Brunswick Street. Joe continued to work away in the lumber camp, and Ola continued to work at Lewis Ltd. He wrote her many love letters while he was away, missing her so very much.

They were happy in the house on Brunswick Street, and lived there several years. Ola missed Joe when he was gone, but she often stopped in to see her parents on her way home from work. She would sometimes eat supper with them, wash the supper dishes and help the children with homework. Ola's father would be lounging on the cot in the big kitchen, chewing tobacco and listening to their conversation. Her mother, always wearing an apron, would sit in the rocking chair by the fire and knit. Sometimes she would undo her long hair, and Ola would brush it for her before braiding it in two long braids and pinning it close to her head.

On a stormy, cold evening, Ola would sometimes walk home with her sisters and spend the night. On a warm evening, following a hot summer day, Ola would sit outside at her own home and talk with the upstairs tenants who found it too hot in their upstairs apartment to remain inside.

Ola's days off would be spent doing laundry. She would get a good fire started early in the morning and heat buckets of water on the wood stove. A large round galvanized tub was brought in from the porch, and the buckets of hot water were poured into it. The clothes were scrubbed, one at a time, against a scrub board. Ola would start washing the dishcloths and towels first, followed by the sheets and pillowcases, then the rest of the whites, leaving the dark clothes until last. Each item had to have the water rung out by hand. Once the clothes were all washed, the water would be emptied outside and clean water poured in the tub. The water for rinsing the clothes was usually not heated, and Ola's hands would be cold and aching, especially in the winter, from ringing the water out of the clothes the second time. An outside clothesline was attached to the house and stretched across the lawn to a large tree at the other end of the yard. Ola would stand on her tiptoes to hang the clothes on the line. Then to keep them from dragging, a pole with a groove in it was pushed against the line to hold it higher up off the ground. Late afternoon, the clothes were brought in off the clothesline. Ola would heat the iron on the stove the next morning and iron everything. In the days before polyester, bed sheets, pillowcases, dish towels, all manner of clothing, and even slips had to be ironed. Or at least the women of the day though it necessary to iron everything. The saying Monday was washday and Tuesday was ironing day wasn't for nothing. In the wintertime, clothes would freeze on the line, and Ola would string them in the kitchen by the wood stove to dry.

Christmas was spent with Ola's family. Ola and Joe had gifts for each other, for her parents and for each sister and brother. Ola had made several batches of fudge and carefully wrapped it for her siblings. They weren't extravagant gifts. Ola told Joe when they were children their mother always made sure they got something. "We would spend the days before Christmas baking cookies. We helped our mother make several batches of bread every week, but it was only on special occasions we made cookies. On Christmas morning there was always an orange in our stocking we had hung the night before. It was the only time of year we got cookies or ate an orange. And homemade mittens. There was always a brand new pair of mittens for each of us."

There was plenty to read in the newspaper in 1936 as the monarchy changed more than once. When King George 5th died at the age of 70, his eldest son was crowned King Edward 8th, but within the year abdicated in order to marry the divorced Wallace Simpson. His brother was crowned King George 6th in December of the same year.

Ma MacInnis passed away in March 1937 after a two-month illness. She was seventy-four. Joe was away working in a lumber camp at the time, and only heard about her passing when he got home two weeks after the funeral. It surprised him that he felt an unexpected lump of sadness for her. She had been a hard woman, and as all British Home Children, he felt pain, even if he didn't understand why he had not been a beloved child. There was a strong

All Alone Again
Joe Payne, British Home Child

social stigma attached to British Home Children, and they were discriminated against. The children were wrongly ashamed of themselves and somehow accepted their fate without question. Even though life with Mrs. MacInnis had been better than if he had stayed in the slums of England, it hurt that he wasn't wanted in his own country and not treated like family in Canada. However, nevertheless, he felt sorry for the life Mrs. MacInnis had lived.

Several of Ola's sisters had beaus and in the summer of 1937, her sister, Jennie got married. The upstairs apartment in Ola and Joe's house had become vacant, and Ola was excited to have her newly married sister move in above them. Although Ola was used to Joe working away, she longed for him to be home with her every night. Jennie's husband Elmo worked for the railway and was home every evening for the supper Jennie had prepared for him. Although they would invite her to join them, Ola didn't like to infringe on their privacy, but she loved having her sister nearby.

The summer of 1938 brought lots of excitement as two more of Ola's sisters, Lillie and Vernie, were getting married, and Jennie was expecting her first child. Ola was excited about the new baby coming, but when Jenny told her Elmo was building them a house in Hilden, not far from the farm where their brother Lawrence lived, she dreaded the thought of them moving away and strangers moving in the apartment above them. The latter wasn't to be because when Vernie got married in August, she and Buster moved in as Jenny and Elmo were moving out.

Ola's father now took in boarders to compensate for the board his daughters would no longer be paying him. During the last few years, he hadn't worked for the town of Truro. The board money he charged his children had been enough to live on.

Ola also had her niece, Marjory, (her sister Prudy's daughter) living with them while Marjory attended Normal College to become a teacher. So, Ola was never completely alone, but still she missed Joe while he was working away.

There had been a political takeover of Germany by Hitler in 1933. Now, in September of 1939, Hitler invaded Poland. Within a couple of days, Britain and France, allies of Poland, declared war on Germany beginning World War 2. Canada joined the Allies along with the US, China, Australia, New Zealand, India and the Soviet

Carolyn MacIsaac

Union. Japan and Italy joined Germany and were known as the Axis. Both Ola's brothers joined the army and fought in the war. However, Joe felt he was getting too old to go to war.

In 1940, Joe was working at a lumber mill in Brookfield. Sitting at the supper table, he remarked offhandedly to Ola, that the land they were logging was for sale. "

I suppose it would be too expensive for us to buy," she offered.

"Well now, it is about two miles from the town, and with the logs cut off the land, it wouldn't be worth much."

So with Ola's encouragement, they were able to buy a large piece of land in Brentwood, just a couple of miles from his work. He was finally able to build the house he had planned on building since he was an eight-year-old boy in England learning to use a hammer for the first time.

The house was small and simply built. It was too far away for Ola to commute to her work at Lewis Ltd. so she became a stay at home housewife. She was excited to have Joe home more often, and at times she would even walk to the woodlot where he was logging.

Ola was quite handy in the kitchen and could whip up a batch of biscuits in minutes. She tried to put some weight on Joe with her homemade biscuits and applesauce, but she often said she was the only one who gained weight.

In 1942, Joe gave a piece of his land to his father-in-law to build their retirement home on. He charged him one dollar to make it legal. They didn't stay neighbors very long. In 1943, Joe and Ola sold their property in Brentwood and bought a small lot of land in the village of Brookfield, closer to his work.

The house in Brentwood had been lit with gas lanterns and candles, but the new house would have electricity. There would be a light hanging from the ceiling in each room and an outlet for Ola to plug in a washing machine, a vacuum cleaner and an iron as soon as Joe could afford to buy them for her. Ola would also be one of the first of her sisters to have an inside toilet. Only her sister Maggie had inside plumbing. Most people, especially those who lived in the country, had outside toilets and made use of the outdated Simpson Sears and Eaton's Catalogues, for toilet paper.

All Alone Again
Joe Payne, British Home Child

This time Joe built a larger two story-house. He had learned a few things from mistakes he had made building the first little house. The new house had two bedrooms and a bathroom upstairs. They hadn't yet had children of their own, but there was always one of Ola's nieces or nephews wanting to spend the night. Her sister Lahlia's daughter, Dorothy, looked forward to spending a week with them every summer. Her sister, Lillie, lived just below her parent's house in Brentwood. Lillie had two small children, Charlie and Barbara. Most every day, Ola walked the two miles to visit her sister and her parents, and to help with the young children. In May of 1945, Lillie had her third child, a baby boy she called Victor.

Joe was always a hard worker. Besides working in the mill and building his house, he also helped his father-in-law build their house. When there was no work at the mill, Joe applied for a job driving a milk truck. The only problem was he didn't have his driver's license. The owners of the dairy allowed this man without a license to take the milk truck to the registry of motor vehicles. Joe jerked the truck back and forth as he tried to steer it, and in the end he was given his driver's license.

So the happy couple lived a contented life in the village of Brookfield. There was a United Church and a store close by. They lived within walking distance to many of Ola's family. They had good neighbours that Ola chatted with daily, and Joe was close to his work. There was only one thing missing. Although Ola loved her nieces and nephews, she longed for a baby of her own.

House in Brookfield

Carolyn MacIsaac

MacInnis/MacKinnon clan (Joe far right, Ola 4th from right)

Cards Joe sent Ola

All Alone Again
Joe Payne, British Home Child

My how you flatters yourself dearie.

Say kid! Betcha a soda that your lips and mine are a perfect fit.

Carolyn MacIsaac

Now I know where they get the ideas for comic Valentines.

We all forgot our troubles at Barney's River, N.S.

Come and join us.

All Alone Again
Joe Payne, British Home Child

Carolyn MacIsaac

Cards to Joe from Ola

Chapter 9

Carolyn (1945)

"Look what we got!" Ola exclaimed as soon as Joe came in the door.

Joe had gone back to work after Christmas at the lumber camp where he worked as a tallyman. Now he had arrived home for New Year's.

Joe and Ola were living in the new house Joe had built on the lane in Brookfield. There was a kitchen, dining room and living room downstairs, and two bedrooms and a bathroom upstairs. Joe had built a small porch on the back of the house, and a veranda across the front which over time he would close in to make a sunporch. He had also built himself a good sized workshop in the backyard.

They were happy, he and Ola. They still lived close enough to her parents and some of her sisters that she could walk to visit them on a daily basis. Ola spent a lot of time with a few of her nieces and nephews. Joe and Ola never had any children of their own. Joe had turned forty in September. Ola was thirty-eight.

Ola led Joe into the living room with a smile on her face. There sat a cradle and inside, a very tiny child, fast asleep.

"Whose baby?" Joe said.

"Our baby, Joe, if we want to keep her," she whispered.

"Who? How?"

"Come out to the kitchen so we don't wake her, and I'll tell you.

"Saturday, I had got dressed, made the bed and came downstairs for the day. It was a nice day for December. I was getting dressed to walk up to Mama's and Papa's. There was a knock on the back door, and when I opened it there was a middle-aged lady there holding this infant baby in her arms. She asked if she could come in. I didn't want her standing there in the cold, so I brought her into the kitchen. I offered to hold the baby while she took her coat off, and hung it on the back of a chair. She followed me into the living room, me still holding the baby. I loosened the blanket around the child as the lady explained her mission.

"The lady told me a story about how this little baby girl's mother was unmarried and unable to keep her. Evidently, the mother has a sister attending teacher's college in Truro, so she came here to have the baby. She found work with Dr. Ross and his wife and lived with them until the baby was born. Then she gave her up for adoption. The girl's father had died before she was born, and there was no way she could take another mouth home for her mother to feed. As it was, her older sister had married, but was now living at home and expecting a new baby herself. Dr. Ross was looking for a home for this infant girl, and spoke with my sister about it. The baby was just ten days old. My sister said that since I wasn't working and had no children of my own perhaps we might take her."

Joe sat just looking at Ola and not saying anything.

"So I told her that I didn't know what you would think, but since she had all the baby's belongings with her, and she didn't know what else to do with the child, I told her I would keep her until you came home and we talked it over."

All Alone Again
Joe Payne, British Home Child

And so Carolyn Anne Atkinson became Carolyn Anne Payne. She was the light of their lives, and they adopted her as soon as they could. Ola wanted to name her Kathleen Edith after her two younger sisters but her mother said that the only thing the poor young woman had to give her baby was the name Carolyn Anne, so they should keep it.

Joe had been a little doubtful at first about having a baby. Times were hard. One night he had an order to make some windows. He stayed up all night to finish them so they could afford to buy milk for the baby.

Visiting Daddy at the lumber camp

The nieces and nephews Ola had spent so much time with, now felt neglected. Her sister Lillie's little girl Barbara, three and a half now, was used to spending quite a lot of time with her Aunt Ola.

"Aunt Ollie," she said, "do you like that broom you're holding?

"Yes Barbie, I like this broom to sweep my floors. Do you not like the broom?"

"No Aunt Ollie. I don't like that broom you're holding, and I don't like that new baby you have either."

Carolyn MacIsaac

Barbie did come to love Carolyn, and they became as close as sisters.

When the weather was nice, Ola pushed Carolyn in the carriage, up the road to her sister Lillie's, and beyond to her parent's home, every day.

Joe had bought his first car, a Morris Minor. He loved to take his wife and daughter for drives around the countryside. One time the back door flew open, and Joe watched in the rearview mirror in horror as Carolyn fell out, and did somersaults on the dirt road. Ola was out of the car before it was fully stopped. Carolyn, not appearing to be hurt in any way, sat up and laughed.

One time, when Ola was visiting her parents, her sister Jennie was also visiting with her two little girls. The little girls, five and seven years older than Carolyn, wanted to go down the lane to visit their cousins, their Aunt Lillie's children, and they wanted to take Carolyn with them.

Ola gave her approval, but watched apprehensively from the window.

Carolyn wasn't sure she wanted to leave her mother, so she started to cry.

Now it so happened that their uncle Tommy was doing some fencing between the two properties. He spotted the girls and asked why Carolyn was crying.

Margie, tugging on Carolyn, responded that the child was wanting to go back with her mother.

Tommy laughed. He knew how his sister doted on the baby she had adopted. "Margie, all that baby needs is a good slap on the bottom."

Margie taking her uncle's advice proceeded to slap Carolyn on the behind.

Carolyn howled!

In seconds, Ola came tearing out of the house, and down the lane. Carolyn would not be visiting her Aunt Lillie without her mother along.

All Alone Again
Joe Payne, British Home Child

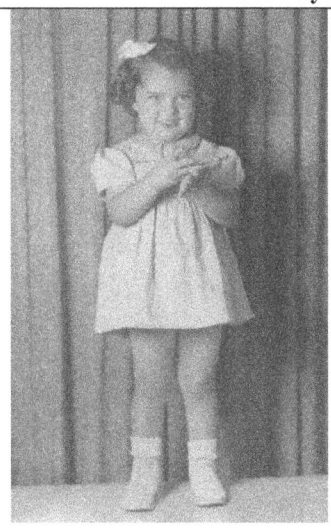

When Carolyn was three and a half, she learned her first lesson, the first that she remembered anyway. She reached through the fence to the neighbour's strawberry patch and picked two beautiful big ripe berries. In order to survive, Joe had stolen a drink of milk when he was a small boy. He had since learned to follow the Ten Commandments. His daughter would never be forced to steal in order to survive if he could help it. She would be taught *Thou Shalt not steal*. Ola immediately marched Carolyn next door, made her apologize, and give the berries back. The kind man told her he appreciated her being honest and hoped she had learned a lesson to never steal. He responded by giving her two whole boxes of berries.

Another time, Carolyn and Stanley, the boy next door, walked up to the highway. Both their mothers were livid. Stanley got a spanking, but Ola felt a scolding sufficed. She knew her daughter would never go near the highway again. The children at the age of four and five were trusted to know their boundaries. In the 1950's it was considered safe to allow children to walk to their neighbours by themselves.

The ice man came to the village every Monday and Thursday morning delivering large blocks of ice. In the days before electricity, the early refrigerators had ice stored inside to keep the perishable food cool. The children gathered around the truck hoping for a small chip of ice to suck on. It was a nice treat on a hot summer day.

Carolyn MacIsaac

Ola persuaded Joe that they should visit the people in Cape Breton where he had been brought up. It bothered her that he had no family. Neil lived in the farmhouse with his wife Mary and their four children. Joe and Ola started a tradition of spending every Labor Day weekend with the MacInnis family in Cape Breton. At first, they took the car across on the ferry, but in 1950 a causeway was built across the strait between the mainland and Cape Breton. The younger MacInnis girl and the two boys were close to Carolyn in age. They became family.

One year the Paynes made an extra trip to Cape Breton at Easter. Easter Sunday, the children got up early and searched all over the house finding colored eggs the bunny had hidden for them. It was fun for Carolyn to join in the activity even though she didn't know the hiding places as well as the three MacInnis children. There were certain things that an only child missed out on.

Another year they went to Cape Breton in July. Beforehand, they picked a couple flats of strawberries and went door to door selling them in remote areas along the way. This paid for their gas, and there were a few boxes left for them to treat the MacInnis family.

Carolyn loved her Dad as much as he loved her. She loved to watch him build things in his workshop. The basics in carpentry that he had learned the year he lived at Middlemore, when he was nine years old, were the beginning of a career as a carpenter. One time Carolyn found an empty aspirin bottle, and half filled it with water. She taped it to a board her father gave her. It is hard to say who was prouder of the level she had made, father or daughter. Joe was a wonderful father. Many British Home Children find it hard to display affection because they were never shown love. Joe experienced love in his earlier years. He was able to show love and accept love.

Once, Carolyn pretended to be a nurse and had her dad's arm in a splint. When unexpected company arrived, he had to explain that there was nothing wrong with his arm.

In 1951, Joe had to travel to Pictou County to find work. He got a job at Eastern Woodworker's, building houses. Not ever wanting to be separated from his family again, he found an apartment for them in Stellarton. They rented out the house in Brookfield at first, but when the job became permanent they sold it and built another one on Munroe Ave. Extension about two miles from Stellarton.

All Alone Again
Joe Payne, British Home Child

  Although Joe worked six days a week, they usually drove to Ola's parents every weekend, sometimes just for the day on Sunday, and sometimes after Joe got home from work on Saturday. There was a store in Mount Thom they often stopped at, and Joe would buy them each a chocolate bar. Eating in a restaurant was only done on a very rare occasion.

  The Paynes had a radio in the kitchen. They often listened to a story on it called "Our Miss Brooks." One evening in February of 1952, when they turned the radio on, they heard that King George V1 had died. His eldest daughter, Elizabeth, was not quite 26 years old. She was crowned Queen Elizabeth the second of England and would become the longest reigning monarch in History.

  Joe loved to treat people. If he was given a box of chocolates he would make them last a long time. When someone visited he would bring out the box and offer them a chocolate. Joe also liked to tease. He told Carolyn that when a baby was born in China, the parents named them by the sound a tin plate made when it landed on the floor, Ping. Clang. Carolyn, believing this story to be true, told her school teacher and classmates about it. Joe played a similar trick on his niece Rosalie while visiting her family in Toronto. He told Rosalie that the blueberries were so large in Ontario that it only took eleven to make a dozen.

  Carolyn never knew if times were hard. It always seemed to her as if she had everything. She always got a new doll for Christmas. The year she turned seven she also asked Santa for a clock. Christmas morning she never let on she was disappointed when she didn't get one. There was a little plastic duck that the child with a great imagination sat on her bedside table, and pretended it was an alarm clock.

  Ola and Joe began to teach their daughter the importance of saving money when she was eight. Carolyn was given $5 for grading into grade four and she opened her first bank account. She was also given $5 every December to buy Christmas presents. She was taught early that it is better to give than to receive. She often gave her mother earrings and her dad a lighter, and she also bought gifts for her grandparents and her cousins. The gifts might be a box of crayons, plastic scissors or a book of lifesavers.

Carolyn MacIsaac

One Christmas when Carolyn asked for a camera, Ola carefully wrapped her own Kodak Box camera and gave it to her daughter. It was many years later that Carolyn wondered if times were hard and her parents couldn't afford everything she asked for, or perhaps they just thought she was too young for the things she wanted.

The winter Carolyn was eight, the three of them had taken the train to Brentwood. There was a station in Brookfield, but the train made an extra stop and let them off in behind Ola's brother Tommy's house. It was starting to snow when Lillie's husband drove them to the station on Sunday for their return trip home on the train. By the time they reached Stellarton, there was a real blizzard. The mother, father and little girl had a tough walk to their home. Joe would walk backwards trying to shelter his wife and daughter from the wind and icy snow pelting their faces. When they reached home, after a long hard hour's walk, the house was cold having no heat. The three of them crawled into one bed exhausted, snuggling to keep warm.

When Carolyn started going skating at the rink on Saturday afternoons, Joe would give her a nickel for candy. Although she sometimes bought sponge taffy, the child who still loves ice-cream would usually buy a fudge stick.

Carolyn loved spending time with her grandparents. Her grandmother always had a quilt set up in the living room that she was quilting, and a mat set up in the spare bedroom, that she was hooking. When not learning how to hook rugs or quilt, Carolyn visited her cousins who lived nearby. Two more of Ola's sisters had built homes across the road from their parents.

One year, when Halloween fell on a Saturday, Joe, Ola and Carolyn spent the night in Brentwood. The adults got dressed up and went trick or treating with the children. Carolyn was used to knocking on a door and being handed some candy. In Brentwood, they only got to about five houses because at each one they would sit for a time while Carolyn's aunts and uncles would try to guess who was hidden behind the masks of their guests.

Carolyn got her first job delivering newspapers on Munroe Avenue Extension when she was eleven years old. Soon after, Joe and Ola realized Carolyn would have to travel to Stellarton for grade

All Alone Again
Joe Payne, British Home Child

seven. They bought a piece of land close to the school in Stellarton and built another house there on Pleasant Street.

House on Pleasant Street

Building a sunporch

Carolyn wasn't able to keep the job delivering newspapers when they moved to Stellarton, but soon after she was once again earning money babysitting.

When she was eleven years old Carolyn started writing to her grandmother in England. After that, every year, her grandmother would send her a small parcel at Christmastime. For several years, one of the gifts was a large hard cover book titled "Girls' Crystal". It contained many short stories about English school girls. Alice still believed that Canada was a big wilderness that didn't have stores that sold books. Her granddaughter would have at least three large hard cover books to read.

Through corresponding with her grandmother, Carolyn learned about her family in England.

***

When she was old enough, Georgina had joined her mother at the factory in Birmingham where they made prams. One evening, in 1936, Georgina had met the man who was to become a major part of her life - Leslie Bumford. A handsome man with a beautiful tan that drew attention, Leslie lived close by on Dudley Road in Winston Green. He had just gotten out of the army after serving for nine years, six of which were served in India on the North West Frontier. Leslie had lied about his age when he had joined the army at the age of 17. When he met Georgina, he was working in a brass foundry making ornamental brass fireplace fenders.

Leslie knew all the tram numbers and where they went in and around the city so on their days off he took Georgina to many different places not far from the city center. Often for a day out they would take a lunch and travel by tram to the beautiful Lickey Hills. It was wonderful to escape the pollution of the city and come to such a magical place where they could breathe fresh air. It was not unusual to see at least one rabbit and usually several deer. It was here a flint arrow head from the Stone Age had been dug up. Although the Burtley lads had the wrong spot, they had told Joe about the arrow head when he had met them while fishing when he was nine years old. In the summertime, Ena and Les might pick berries to go with their lunch. In the fall everything was purple with heather. In wintertime, the Lickey Hills became a winter wonderland. They would take a sled with them and coast down the hills.

Georgina and Leslie were married on July 28[th,] 1937. He was 26 and she was 27. Alice stood for them. They were as happy as they

All Alone Again
Joe Payne, British Home Child

could be, living in hard times, in Birmingham, during The Industrial Revolution.

When the Second World War broke out in 1939, Leslie was still on the reserve to the Devonshire regiment. He and Georgina went to the market in the Bull Ring where he bought a new shirt, went into the toilets and changed into the new shirt, came out and they walked together to New Street train station. Leslie gave Georgina a kiss goodbye and away to war he went.

Alice was not going to live in Birmingham through another war. She was determined that her daughter would not live there either, awaiting a husband who might never return. So the two of them left the huge polluted city and returned to Blockley where Alice had lived as a child and still had connections with Lady Churchill. They took very few of their belongings with them. They caught the train from Birmingham to Honeybourne, then cycled the remainder of the way, which was about fifteen miles.

The little cottage on Bell lane was small but adequate. After living in one room during the war, Alice was happy to have a front room, bedroom and a kitchen. There was even a small porch attached. Alice had enough money saved to buy an old treadle Singer sewing machine, and was able to make a living, sewing and selling children's clothes. She walked to the surrounding hamlets and villages selling baby's and children's clothes throughout the 1940's and 1950's.

Alice was happy to be back in Blockley. One day, after much begging from some old friends, she bicycled with them into the beautiful Cotswold Hills. On this beautiful day, they had taken a bottle of cold tea and a jam sandwich wrapped in newspaper for a picnic lunch and sat on the grass overlooking the Vale of Evesham. They could see in the distance, Gloucestershire County, God's wonderful country, and to the west the Black Mountains in South Wales.

Alice was lost in thought as she breathed in the fresh air and looked over the beautiful countryside. There was green everywhere, trees and grass among the cottages built of honey colored stone along the narrow cobbled streets. There were flowers too, in the yards and in the fields, and spectacular rose bushes climbing up the front of the houses. It was a charming sight found nowhere else in the world. She couldn't help but compare it to the city life in the overcrowded

Birmingham, with smog so thick you couldn't see through it. And, thinking of Joe, who was still often in her thoughts, she gazed, lost in thought, towards the west.

When the war was over in 1945, Leslie had stayed on in the Military police for a few months moving prisoners, and then came to Blockley when he was demobbed. Alice moved into Lady Northwick Homes, not far from Leslie and Georgina who moved to a place on Station Road. A year later their son was born, a baby boy, named Joey after the brother Georgina had lost to another country.

***

When Carolyn was in grade nine, Ola persuaded Joe to take out some insurance money they had saved and go to England. He went by plane this time, and spent a month with his mother and sister.

It was nice to visit England, but his mum and sister, with their strong Cotswold accent, seemed like strangers to him. A half century had passed. The small boy was a grown man in his 50's and the young mother was now a grey haired lady in her 70's. Joe's mother didn't often talk about the situation that led her to lose one of her children. They didn't take Joe around and introduce him to anyone, and Joe presumed he didn't have any other relatives, until one day he was at the bank, and the teller told him they were cousins.

Alice was relieved that her son was doing so well and had prospered. She told only her closest friend. "Imagine having money to fly all the way from Canada to England to see us. He was very kind to us. He purchased food and things to make us more comfortable and got all kinds of little trinkets to take back to his wife and daughter in Canada". Joe had purchased new linoleum to replace the badly worn floor in his mother's porch. Joe had even invited his mother to come live with them in Canada. Alice didn't know that her son and his wife were willing to sleep in the sunporch in order to give his mother a bedroom. But, Alice couldn't leave Ena, and little Joey. Ena needed her. Joe had made Canada his home. She was happy for him and could finally let him go.

Ena's husband, Leslie, made sure Joe saw a bit of the countryside while he visited them. Blockley, lying in a valley on the edge of the north Cotswolds, was only one of many villages in a rural area of south central England. Its rolling hills and a grassland harbour

All Alone Again
Joe Payne, British Home Child

covered parts of six counties known as the Cotswolds. The Cotswold Way ran over one hundred miles along the escarpment edge from Chipping Campden to Bath. The Cotswolds with its thatched medieval villages, churches and stately homes of honey colored limestone was home to some of the most unspoilt, historic and famous towns and villages in England. The North Cotswolds were known for having some of the finest churches in the world built by very wealthy wool merchants. These little villages were just a five or ten minute drive away. One special place Leslie showed him was Shakespeare's Birthplace in Stratford-on-Avon.

When the month was up, Joe was more than happy to come back to Canada, to his family, his wife and his daughter, and Ola's family. Ola's family had become his family. Alice was sad to see her son leave but his coming to see her had given her a sort of peace. Her baby boy was a grown man and had surpassed her greatest desires for him. He had a wife, a daughter, a nice house and a job. His life was in Canada. Hers was in England.

***

In 1964 Carolyn got married and moved to Toronto. Finding separation difficult again, Joe quit his job at the Casket Factory where he was now working. He and Ola sold the house in Stellarton and most of their belongings. They moved to Toronto to be near their

Carolyn MacIsaac

daughter. Joe and Ola got a job as superintendents in an apartment building, and Carolyn and Eldridge moved into one of the apartments.

They loved being near their daughter, but Ola missed her family. After two years, while home visiting Nova Scotia, they bought 90 acres of land in the country, not far from Pictou. Joe was not quite old enough to get the old age pension, so he took a job working as a flagman for the department of highways. He started building a garage that they could live in temporarily until he got a house built. Ola thought it was so big it might as well be the house. What was started as a garage ended up a small one bedroom bungalow. A kitchen had to be added to it and eventually a front and back porch. This was the fifth and last house Joe built for them to live in.

For a time, Joe drove his nephew Bob to work in the mornings.

"What time do you start work, Uncle Joe"?

"7 AM."

"Well then how come you go an hour early?'

"Well, you see Bob, you just never know when you might have a flat tire."

That was the hardworking, conscientious man Joe was.

Joe, although very generous to others, was always very frugal with money. He sold the wood off the property in Durham for what he had paid for the land.

By 1967, Carolyn was missing her parents, so she and Eldridge moved back to Nova Scotia. They found an apartment in Stellarton, and a year later built a home in Durham on Joe's land.

Joe's House in Durham

All Alone Again
Joe Payne, British Home Child

The MacInnis girls in front of Joe's house in Durham: Hughena, Mary, Jessie, Mary Sarah, Alena (missing Christine)

News from England

Joe's Mum lived in Lady Northwick Homes until June 1965. She then moved in with her daughter so she could be looked after in her old age.

Carolyn MacIsaac

Alice and Ena, 13 Station Rd. Blockley, August 11, 1968

Death of Joe's Mum at the age of 89

    One time, Carolyn, her husband, and their three little children spent a night in Halifax at the Bayview Motel in Fairview. They didn't know it at the time, but the owners of the motel had bought the

152

All Alone Again
Joe Payne, British Home Child

land where the Middlemore Home had once stood. The motel incorporated the Middlemore Home and remodeled it. It is possible, that Carolyn's little children put their hand on the railing of the staircase, in the exact spot their nine-year-old grandfather had put his little hand, on his first day in Canada sixty years earlier.

Staircase at the Bayview Motel in Fairview

Joe delighted in his grandchildren. He saw Carolyn and her three children, two girls and a boy, every day. He and Ola had a busy contented life. They bought yarn at the carpet factory, and worked together knitting and hooking mats when they weren't on the road visiting Ola's family.

Joe also loved going to card parties, and often came home with a blanket or something he had won. He attended card parties regularly until he was hospitalized for lung cancer on Christmas Day in 1986. He died on Valentine's Day 1987 at the age of 81.

Joe had never spoken of his earlier struggles; what it felt like to be torn from his mother, his sister, his homeland; what it felt like to live in an orphanage, to travel across the vast ocean in a rocking ship

Carolyn MacIsaac

meant to hold cattle; what it felt like to live with a family who didn't speak English, in a freezing cold house in winter, and to be expected to work like a man when he was only nine years old.

Joe had lost his beloved Ola on August 10, 1977.

Six little words he had spoken on the way home from her funeral spoke volumes.

"Now I am all alone again!"

He spent the last ten years of his life, alone again, in the little house in Durham.

Epilogue

Joe Payne, not only survived but like most of the British Home Children, he prospered. You can see from all the postcards he received over the years that he was loved. He was a very easy going, kind, gentle man. He worked hard. He was happy.

The following pages are newspaper articles about celebrating British Home Child Day in Nova Scotia and Canada, proclaiming October as The Month of the Home Child, a postage stamp to honor British Home Children, planting trees in memory of British Home Children across the province, and placing benches and plaques in memory of Home Children. There is a silk lilac tree planted outside the McCulloch House in Pictou to honor my dad, Joseph Payne, and other British Home Children who settled in Pictou County. In front of the tree, there is a bench to sit on and remember our loved ones.

Towards the end, there is an article about a moment long awaited by British Home Children and their descendants, an apology from Ottawa, and on March 7th. 2018, our Federal government declared September 28th of each year to be named "British Home Child Day."

Stamp to honor British Home Children

Carolyn MacIsaac

Nova Scotia
Proclamation
Month of the British Home Children

WHEREAS there is a long legacy of British Home Children coming to our province - children orphaned, impoverished, abandoned or illegitimate - sent to be cared for in Canada; and

WHEREAS in 2009, surviving British Home Children will be commemorating 140 years of these young British subjects leaving their country to live with complete strangers in Canada - a journey which would have been a frightening prospect for children as young as four years of age; and

WHEREAS while many of these children were welcomed into homes and families across our province and country, others lived through great hardship, ostracization and uncertainty; and

WHEREAS the descendants of these British Home Children plan special celebrations during 2009;

THEREFORE be it resolved that I, Rodney J. MacDonald, Premier of Nova Scotia, do hereby proclaim October, 2009, as "Month of the British Home Children" in the Province of Nova Scotia

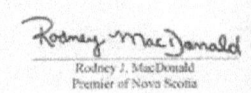

Rodney J. MacDonald
Premier of Nova Scotia

Signed at Halifax, Nova Scotia

Trees to be planted in memory of British Home Children

By MONICA GRAHAM

When Carolyn MacIsaac plants a tree at the Hector Exhibit Centre in Pictou in October, she'll think about her father.

Joseph Payne was one of more than 100,000 British children shipped to Canada between 1869 and the 1930s, at least 6,000 of them to the Maritimes.

Called the Child Emigration Scheme, the plan removed orphans and impoverished children from communities all over Britain and sent them to Canada where many were settled with farm families as labourers and servants. Some were as young as four, and many were bounced from home to home.

They are now known as the British Home Children, and they account for the parentage of about 10 per cent of Canada's population.

"A lot of them came around 1914, like Dad," Ms. MacIsaac said Saturday.

Mr. Payne went to a farm in Cape Breton and then on to Truro when he was 18. He later moved to Durham, near Pictou.

It's doubtful any British Home Children are still alive to attend the Oct. 10 tree-planting ceremony, but Ms. MacIsaac hopes their descendants will. She's tracked down 13 in the local area, and more live across Nova Scotia, she said.

Descendants tried to have 2009 declared the Year of the British Home Children, she said. That was done in New Brunswick, but Nova Scotians were assigned only the month of October, she said. Events include an Oct. 17 reunion in Sydney and an exhibit in Truro starting Oct. 12.

"In the past few years, there's been a reunion in Truro," Ms. MacIsaac said.

She's looking for other descendants of British Home Children to share their stories at the tree-planting ceremony, set for 10 a.m. Contact carolynmacisaac@eastlink.ca or the Hector Exhibit Centre at pcghs@gov.ns.ca.

(mgraham@herald.ca)

RELIVE THE MEMORIES

All Alone Again
Joe Payne, British Home Child

Home Children

October 2009 has been declared Month of the British Home Child in Nova Scotia. In Pictou County, we are recognizing the Home Children by planting a tree in their honour in front of the Hector Centre. We expect many of the British Home Children descendants in our area and some from outside Pictou County to be there when we plant an ivory silk lilac at 10 a.m. Saturday, Oct. 10. The public is invited.

Charlie Parker, MLA for Pictou West, will be there to speak. We have also invited Immigration Minister Ramona Jennex and Percy Paris, the minister of Tourism, Culture and Heritage. The Hector Centre is providing a plaque to recognize British Home Children who immigrated to Canada from the Barnardo and Middlemore homes in England. We will be registering our tree with the United Nations Environment Program: Billion Tree Campaign.

Between 1869 and the 1930s, more than 100,000 children who were orphaned, impoverished, abandoned or illegitimate were sent to be cared for in Canada. More than 50 agencies were involved, and received $2 per child. Children between the ages of three and 16 were brought to Canada, often on ships that were used to take cattle to England and would otherwise be empty. These young British subjects left their country to live with complete strangers in Canada and were indentured until age 18. Some were welcomed into homes and families and some survived great hardships. Today, their descendants make up 12 per cent of Canadians.

Other events taking place include the British Home Children and Descendants Association's seventh annual reunion in Sydney on Oct. 17; and the Colchester Historical Museum in Truro has set up a commemorative display which will run until the end of October. Members of the British Home Children and Descendants Association remain hopeful that their request will be granted to have 2009 declared Year of the British Home Child by both the federal and provincial governments, in this the 140th year since this emigration scheme began.

Carolyn MacIsaac, British Home Child descendant, Pictou

Carolyn MacIsaac

Tree and Bench at McCulloch House in Pictou, June 2018

All Alone Again
Joe Payne, British Home Child

Canada's children of the empire
Thousands of British home children sent to Canada were treated like servants
By HEATHER LASKEY

A group of Barnardo boys and girls arrive in Nova Scotia in 1921.

In 2010 Stephen Harper announced that he would not be making an apology. But, then on February 16, 2017

Ottawa - It was a moment long-awaited by British Home Children and their descendants.

On February 16, 2017 the Canadian House of Commons passed a motion, formally apologizing to the children uprooted through the long-standing migration program.

From 1869 to the end of the 1940s, 55 agencies in Great Britain sent more than 100,000 children to Canada, to work as indentured farm workers and domestics. Uprooted from their mother country, separated from surviving family members, most of the children were used as a supply of cheap labour – and many suffered abuse, stigma and neglect.

Luc Theriault, Bloc Quebecois MP for Montcalm, PQ put forward the motion, "That the House recognize the injustice, abuse and suffering endured by the British Home Children as well as the efforts, participation and contribution of these children and their descendants within our communities; and offer its sincere apology to the British Home Children who are still living and to the descendants of these 100,000 individuals who were shipped from Great Britain to Canada between 1869 and 1948, and torn from their families to serve mainly as cheap labour once they arrived in Canada."

Theriault was supported by MPs Judy Sgro (Humber River-Black Creek; Liberal), Mark Strahl (Chilliwack-Hope; Conservative), Jenny Kwan (Vancouver East; NDP) and Elizabeth May (Saanich-Gulf Islands; Green).

In Canada, British Home Children and their descendants are estimated to make up 10 to 12% of the population, or nearly 4 million Canadians. Among the children sent to Quebec was John James Rowley – father of Hélène Rowley, who married Jean Duceppe and had 7 children, including Gilles Duceppe, former Bloc Quebecois leader and MP.

"I am very happy that all the parties have joined together today to apologize, as did Australia and the United Kingdom, to the British Home Children," Duceppe said following the announcement.

Australia issued its apology in 2009, when Prime Minister Kevin Rudd spoke of "the tragedy, the absolute tragedy of childhoods lost." The UK apologized on behalf of the British government in 2010. In Canada, the government declined to respond to calls for an apology - until now.

Advocates are delighted with the news. Sandra Joyce, co-founder of British Home Child Group International (britishhomechild.com) and a British Home Child descendant, called it "truly an exciting moment for the British Home Children still with us and their descendants... Their stories, largely unknown until now because of the stigma they faced in Canada, are part of the diverse tapestry that makes up our great nation." She expressed a hope that the acknowledgement will lead to "more reunions of families torn apart by this child migrant scheme." *

- Sandra Joyce Author and Co-founder of the British Home Child Group International

All Alone Again
Joe Payne, British Home Child

Proclamation February 7, 2018

On March 7th, 2018, our Federal government declared September 28th. of each year to be named "British Home Child Day".

Private Members' Business   5:30 p.m
Acadie—Bathurst New Brunswick   Liberal

Serge Cormier Parliamentary Secretary to the Minister of Immigration

Mr. Speaker, I am pleased to rise in the House today to speak to Motion No. 133, which seeks to declare September 28 of every year British home child day in Canada.

This motion seeks to recognize the significant contributions that the British home children made to Canada, especially their service to our armed forces throughout the 20th century.

The motion also seeks to recognize the hardships and stigmas that many of the British home children endured, as well as the importance of educating and reflecting upon their story for future generations.

I fully support this motion, and I urge my parliamentary colleagues to do the same. We should all be proud to recognize the contributions made by these people, who came to Canada as children and helped build our country.

It is estimated that 12% of Canadians have ancestors who were British home children. That is approximately 4 million people, an incredible number. In other words, one Canadian in nine. The thinking that led to the decision to uproot those children from their lives in England and send them to another country, thousands of kilometres away, seems absurd to us today. The children had no idea what awaited them. The story of their lives in Canada is happy for some and sad for others. Moreover, the background of a large number of them will forever remain unknown. Many were initially ashamed and, once they were adults, they decided to forget. They have never told their families how things went after they arrived in Canada.

Others know nothing about their families and heritage because, in some cases, the charitable organizations that brought them to Canada changed their names. They were so young when it happened, and they no longer remember their birth names or who their biological parents were. David and Kay Lorente from Renfrew, Ontario, were among the first to stand up for the rights of home children and their family members. They founded Home Children Canada, which has helped many families gain access to personal files and has raised awareness in Canada about British home children.

David's father was a home child who, by all accounts, had a difficult time at the first farm where he was placed, but who was treated well at the second.

I would be remiss if I did not also mention the efforts that Perry Snow, John Willoughby, and Lori Oschefski have made to ensure that this important part of Canadian history is never forgotten.

The children who arrived in Canada came from all over the United Kingdom. Some of them were orphans. However, many of them had families and, for various poverty-related reasons, were placed in institutions, likely workhouses, correctional facilities, or homes run by charitable organizations.

At the time, governments on both sides of the Atlantic considered immigration of that kind to be a good idea. In the 1860s, England went through an economic depression and sending children to Canada allowed the government to divest itself of the costs of meeting their needs.

Correspondingly, Canada was expanding and farms all across the country were desperately seeking labour. Initially, the children's travel expenses were greatly subsidized in Canada. Nova Scotia provided $5 for young children and $10 for older ones. Ontario provided $6 and

All Alone Again
Joe Payne, British Home Child

the federal government provided $2 for every child that the charitable organizations brought into the country.

Once the children arrived in Canada, the charitable organizations reached apprenticeship agreements in order to stabilize the working conditions of children of various ages. For the young children, the organizations gave about $5 per month in compensation to the family caring for them, whereas older children were expected to work for a living.

Most organizations required children over the age of 14 to be paid a salary for the work that they did. However, many children never received that salary and, for the majority of them, their lives were defined by the work they could do rather than by what they needed.

In fact, the apprenticeship agreements are brutal reminders that the children were not considered to be family members, but servants. What situation did the children find themselves in? It is impossible to know for sure. There is very little data available. However, by collecting letters, archives, and evidence from various inquiries held in the United Kingdom and Australia, a reasonable picture can be painted, a picture of a very difficult life that, for some, brought much suffering.

We need to recognize the pain associated with the loss of their identity, as well as the fact that some of the children were abused. This event is part of Canada's history, and we must recognize its existence today. However, many Canadians are unaware of this chapter of our country's history. I myself did not know about this story.

By declaring September 28 British Home Child Day, we send a powerful message about the importance of the personal and collective experience these children went through and the role they played in building our country.

Not only did they help build this country, they also fought to keep it free. An estimated 10,000 British home children fought for Canada in World War I. Many also fought in World War II alongside the

Carolyn MacIsaac

descendants of children who came to Canada at the beginning of the immigration program.

The government has supported several awareness, commemoration, and education initiatives to highlight the many hardships British home children experienced and their contribution to Canada.

The partnership between Library and Archives Canada and the British Isles Family History Society of Greater Ottawa is one of the most important initiatives. Thanks to this partnership, extensive records held by Library and Archives Canada on the British home children have been publicly released, and most of them are also available online. These records include passenger lists, immigration branch correspondence files, inspection reports, non-government collections, and indexes to some records held in the United Kingdom.

I am certain that my colleagues will vote in favour of this motion and that the British home children will get the recognition they deserve.

Once this motion is adopted, Canadians will want to learn more about this unique event in our shared history and the contributions that British home children and their descendants have made to our country. Once again, I hope my colleagues in the House will vote yes on this motion.

Statements By Members February 7th, 2018 / 2:15 p.m.

Conservative

Guy Lauzon Stormont—Dundas—South Glengarry, ON

This evening, hon. members of the House will have the opportunity to vote on my private member's Motion No. 133, which aims to establish a British home child day in Canada, to be celebrated yearly on September 28.

All Alone Again
Joe Payne, British Home Child

Until recent years, very few Canadians knew about the British home children. Their stories of hardship, courage, determination, and perseverance are not part of Canadian history books. This needs to change.

Eleanor McGrath, a constituent of mine, has released a wonderful documentary called *Forgotten*. I encourage everyone to watch it on TVO this coming February 22, at 9 p.m.

We owe a great deal to these children for their contributions to our country. So far, we have been failing them. I encourage all members to make an effort to learn more about the story of the British home children, to share that knowledge with their constituents, and to do all they can to ensure that this chapter of their collective story is never forgotten.

Nova Scotia's new British Home Children monument was installed at Terminal Road, Halifax, December 11, 2018. It is situated near the main entrance to Pier 21.

Carolyn MacIsaac

Acknowledgements

I have been attending British Home Children reunions for the past eighteen years. The members have been helpful in getting me many copies of records pertaining to my dad. I thank each of you who have helped and encouraged me over the years. .

I have also taken notes from all the guest speakers over the years. I wish I had written down all the names to give them credit. Without them I wouldn't have a book.

I also want to thank all the authors of the books I have read. I have listed some below and am sorry for the ones I am missing. If you are reading this, thank you to each and every one of you.

An Alphabetic list of just a few of the British Home Children books I have read:

Awful Kind by Sarah Underwood
Charlie: a Home Child's Life in Canada by Beryl Young
Empty Cradles by Margaret Humphreys
Great Canadian Expectations, the Middlemore Experience by Dr. Patricia Roberts-Pichette
Marjory Too Afraid to cry by Patricia Skidmore
Middlemore Memories – Tales of the British Home Children by Michael Staples
The Little Immigrants by Kenneth Bagnell
The Street Arab – The Story of a British Home Child by Sandra Joyce

Two sites on Facebook:

British Home Children and Descendants Association (Nova Scotia)
Families of British Home Children / British Child Migrants